Anna B. Hoppe

Her Life and Hymnody

Elisabeth Joy Urtel

Lutheran University Press
Minneapolis, Minnesota

Anna B. Hoppe
Her Life and Hymnody

Elisabeth Joy Urtel, author

This monograph is adapted from a master's thesis submitted on April 13, 2016, to Bethany Lutheran Theological Seminary, Mankato, Minnesota in partial fulfillment of the requirements for the degree, Master of Arts in Lutheran Theological Studies.

Published under the auspices of:
Center for Church Music
Concordia University Chicago
River Forest, IL 60305-1402

ISBN: 978-1-942304-33-3

Supplemental to this printed monograph, the Center for Church Music has published on its website the complete texts to Anna Hoppe's hymns.

Go to https://cuchicago.edu/about-concordia/center-for-church-music and click on "Research." then on either "Anna Hoppe—*Songs for the Church Year*" or "Anna Hoppe—Hymns printed in *The Northwestern Lutheran* and *The Lutheran Companion* (1914-1941)."

Lutheran University Press
PO Box 390759
Minneapolis, MN 55439
Manufactured in the United States of America

Contents

About the Center
for Church Music

The Center for Church Music was established in 2010 on the campus of Concordia University Chicago. Its purpose is to provide ongoing research and educational resources in Lutheran church music, especially in the areas of congregational song and composition for the Church. It is intended to be of interest to pastors, musicians, and laity alike.

The Center maintains a continually expanding resource room that houses the Schalk American Lutheran Hymnal Collection, the manuscript collections of prominent Lutheran composers and hymn writers, and a broad array of reference works and resources in church music. To create a global awareness and facilitate online research, efforts are underway to digitize the hymnal collection, the manuscript archives, and the hymn festival recordings.

The Center publishes monographs and books covering various aspects of Lutheran church music.

The Center maintains a dynamic website whose features include devotions, presentations, oral histories, biographical essays, resource recommendations, and conversations on various topics in worship and church music.

The Center's Founders Group includes Linda and Robert Kempke, Nancy and Bill Raabe, Mary and Charles Sukup, and Waldemar B. Seefeldt, whose significant monetary gifts initiated the Center and have, along with the gifts of many others, sustained its momentum.

The Center's Advisory Board includes James Freese, Scott Hyslop, Linda Kempke, Jonathan Kohrs, Nancy Raabe, Carl Schalk, Steven Wente, and Paul Westermeyer.

Barry L. Bobb serves as the Center's volunteer director.

You can follow news about the Center on Facebook. Learn more about the Center and subscribe to its free e-newsletter at http://cuchicago.edu/about-concordia/center-for-church-music

Publisher's Preface

During the last forty years English-speaking Christians the world over have been blessed by an "explosion" of original hymnody. Lutheran hymn writers in the United States have been an important part of that phenomenon. Their work has been so pervasive that a roll call of names comes easily to mind—Martin Franzmann, Gracia Grindal, Herb Brokering, Jaroslav Vajda, John Ylvisaker, Herman Stuempfle, Susan Cherwien, Stephen Starke and many others. Even though some of these are now sainted, their Spirit-led creative outpouring remains very much alive among us. Their words of faith still flow forth from our mouths in our weekly worship. Their insightful texts still help to form and express our faith daily, often in ways beyond our knowing. We know them and their work well because so much has been written about them—background stories in denominational magazines, collections of their hymns, profile videos and interviews, biographies and the like. We know these sisters and brothers well.

But, of course, this has not always been the case. Renown and popularity have seldom surrounded the hymn writers of the Church. Many, if not most, do their labor of love in almost complete obscurity. Certainly, this was the case with Anna B. Hoppe, one of the most prolific Lutheran hymn writers of the early 20th century. She composed hundreds of hymns along with opinion pieces and devotional writing. All the while, she lived quietly in Milwaukee, working as an office secretary and volunteering in various roles at her church. Despite her humble life, she became acquainted with several important Lutheran church musicians and pastors of her day and they, impressed by her work, helped to "spread the news" about her remarkable achievements. Today Lutherans still know her through just a few of her hymns—"O Son of God, in Galilee" (LSB 841, LW 400, LBW 426), "For Jerusalem You're Weeping" (LW 390), and "Rise, Arise" (CW 30). Hoppe's major collection, *Songs of the Church Year: Hymns on the Gospel and Epistle Texts and Other Songs* (published in 1928 by Augustana Book Concern, 334 pages in hard cover) is still listed on amazon.com, but copies are scarce. [The full text of this collection can be found on the website for the Center for Church Music, under its "Research" feature.]

This is why Elisabeth Urtel's exhaustive research and insightful analysis are so important. She brings to light an important time in American Lutheranism and the spiritual leadership of a remarkable woman. You will find in these pages two inspiring stories of perseverance. One is the broader context of Lutherans in America finding their way, making the transition to English, enduring the suspicions of Germans during World War I, most of its members just getting by in hard times. Singled out is the story of Anna Hoppe, unmarried and living with her family, having only a grade school education, working in menial jobs, and serving in her church. But, all the while, also keeping up with the larger issues of the day and of Christianity in the world and finding creative expression of her deeply felt faith in original poems which she humbly offered to the wider Church.

Anna remains a model for all who care about the Church and its music in our own day.

Barry L. Bobb

Introduction

"Why not original American Lutheran hymns? Are we so super critical as to stifle originality in our Church?"

While church musicians, hymnologists, translators, pastors, theologians, and laypeople may consider this issue settled in our day (given the full flowering of American Lutheran congregational song in the last 40 years), that was not the case in the early years of the 20th century. This question was urgently raised in 1919 by Dr. Adolf Hult, professor at Augustana Theological Seminary (Rock Island, Illinois). In an article entitled "The Future American Lutheran Hymnbook" for the *Lutheran Companion*[1], the professor aired his yearning for a revolution of uniquely Lutheran hymnody, culminating in a single hymnal. This goal of one common worship book had circulated since the time of Henry Melchior Muhlenberg (1711-87), the patriarch of Lutheranism in the United States. He wrote in the preface to the *Erbauliche Lieder-Sammlung* (1786), the first intentionally American-Lutheran hymnal, "If only there were one hymnbook for all American congregations that would contain the best of the old and new spiritual songs, how much more convenient and harmonious it would be."[2]

Compiling a hymnal solely of Lutheran hymns, including treasures translated from the German and Scandinavian languages as well as American-English offerings, and distributing it in every synod could have a profound influence on doctrine and practice. On the other hand, if done hastily or indiscreetly, the work could destroy the confessional Lutheran movement. If assembled with an eye for orthodox hymnody, however, it could enrich and unify all its members, stimulating the creative output of writers and musicians alike. By a "universal Lutheran hymnbook for America," Hult envisions an anthology not simply compiled by a Lutheran committee but representing the heritage of European hymnists via translation and selecting the best of the Reformation songs. Yet, most significantly, contemporary Lutheran names would appear increasingly beside those of the Reformers in the hymnal contents, showing that the creative spring, empowered by Holy Spirit, had continued uninterrupted.

Nevertheless, a synod or congregation could not easily collectively accomplish this task. It would have to start at a personal level, with sound Lutheran hymnwriters. They would have to pen hymns which not only acknowledge the past gems of Martin Luther, Paul Gerhardt, Johann Heermann, and others, but also address the present needs of the Church and the tradition's future heirs. Such an individual effort could activate a hymnic reformation by example, furnishing others with an appreciation of church music the will to create a model of how it might be carried out. Early 20th-century Lutheranism, as it endured rising levels of tension regarding hymn selection and usage, was lying in wait for such a model, whether it realized it or not.

Yet, what if a model had already come, and drifted by essentially unnoticed? While others gathered near the active modern press to hear a distinctive American-Lutheran voice of hymnody, perhaps it already existed— tucked away in worn newspapers, typewritten letters, unsung musical scores, and a solitary but remarkable collection of hymns. The writer of such a collection echoed Hult's sentiment around fifteen years later, in 1934:

> At present a committee is at work compiling an English Hymnal to be used by the entire Synodical Conference. Will the time ever come when all American Lutherans "sing themselves together"? Our American Lutheran hymnody might reach the sublime heights obtained by the old masters, who were so filled with the wells of Living Water that their hearts overflowed, who gathered honey of the Rock and sweetened all they came in contact with, but they are "calling back" to us as the poet says, to "help our feet along the stony track" and if, with hearts attuned to the brooding of God's Spirit, and pens dipped

in prayer, the Lord gives us American writers to answer the call, we may some day have the American Lutheran harp of many strings, which Dr. Hult pleaded for in an article in *The Lutheran Companion* some years ago. God grant him the desire of his heart! And if the Giver of every good and perfect gift grants me grace to become even the humblest of these strings, it will be my delight to show forth the praises of His Unspeakable Gift, my Lord and Saviour, to Whom be glory in the Church now and forever.[3]

This "harp string," a Wisconsin Synod Lutheran named Anna Bernardine Dorothy Hoppe, was not frequently heard at the time, but this was not because her hymnic voice was "out of tune." A Milwaukee native, daughter, sister, secretary, columnist, and poet, Anna may be the most prolific American-Lutheran hymnwriter of the 20th century. Her myriad of original Gospel and Epistle hymns as well as translations from German, beginning with appearances in *The Northwestern Lutheran* (later *Forward in Christ*[4]), ultimately consummated in a collection— *Songs for the Church Year* (1928). As we contemplate the shape of original Lutheran hymnody in the 21st century, a new study of Anna's life and hymnody is well worth our time.

Through this reflection on Anna's Christian vocation and her poems, the author desires to encourage two responses:

1. First of all, the awareness to recognize the God-sent blessings of Anna's hymnody and its impact upon the Wisconsin Synod, the Augustana Synod, the Synodical Conference, and modern Lutheran hymnody. During her lifetime many Augustana Lutherans sang her poetry regularly from their *Hymnal and Order of Service* (1925), and subscribers to Wisconsin's *The Northwestern Lutheran* eagerly awaited each new poem. Through her hymnody, she established edifying relationships with a variety of people across the country, from respected musicians to influential pastors.

2. Also, the author hopes to encourage a new movement of Lutheran hymnody based on the model Anna provided in her

Songs for the Church Year. Though having only a day-school education, Anna learned to write through practical experience with hymnody. Allotted but short recesses at work, she wisely managed her time around secretarial duties, church involvement, and other activities to compose hymns, writing them by hand or her desk typewriter. With the target of producing one thousand new hymns, encompassing every season of the liturgical calendar, she came close to that goal, motivated by love of congregational song, her church, and the need for doctrinally solid Lutheran texts.

Shown how it can be done utilizing colorful literary mastery and a faithful application of Biblical truths, other Christians could note carefully and also contribute in their own way to the hymnody of the Church and all the Lutheran arts in like manner. Complementing the historic readings for each Sunday and festival, a hymn unwrapping their context, characters, settings, motives, and purpose remains a worthy and constructive idea. Hymns aligning with the liturgical rhythm of the Christian year reinforce the themes of the day, enough to carry the churchgoer through the week. More could be written about the use of the Hymn of the Day—as devotions at home, or even for personal enjoyment in the appreciation of Christian poetry. Continuing this theme, what if visual artists were to provide art to supplement these songs, illuminating each of the lessons for use in church or home decoration? Entwining the fine arts would highlight the Scriptural message and help to secure its remembrance.

While Anna's hymns are specifically Biblical, they are also correspondingly Lutheran in understanding. In them, Christ Jesus is the incarnate second person of the Trinity, possessing a fully divine and fully human nature, the former sharing all characteristics with the latter. (Colossians 2:9) By his perfect life and death on the cross, he ransomed, pardoned, redeemed, justified, atoned, and saved every human being from damnation, declaring them righteous (Romans 5:1). Viewed through the atoning lens of Christ's work, God considers sinners to be saints (Colossians 1:22), sharing in all of the privileges of the Son (Ephesians 1:3). Through the means of grace, the Word and the Sacraments, believers receive strength to endure on earth as citizens of the eternal kingdom until they come into their inheritance. This is the heart of Anna's poetic theology. While others liken her voice to that of Frances Havergal[5] (as noted later), we hear a distinctively different tone—not that of a Reformed-American songbird, but rather a German-Lutheran nightingale, nesting anew in the friendly shade of Wisconsin.

If a telling song such as this endures, why must it go unheard? It carries with it the theology of the Lutheran faith, the charm of a woman's perspective, and an example of vocation for all. By re-opening the pages of Anna Hoppe's *Songs for the Church Year* and unfolding the time-worn leaves of *The Northwestern Lutheran*, 21st century Christians will be enriched by her simple, energetic poetry, rich in Scriptural imagery and hymnic language. The story of these gifts begins in Milwaukee—in a Lutheran home, a landmark Wisconsin Synod congregation, and not far from the heart of the Synodical Conference's activity.

Elisabeth Joy Urtel

Anna B. Hoppe

Biographical Background

Anna's Early Years (1889-1914)

Family Life in Milwaukee

If one was not of German descent, the culture of 1880s Milwaukee might have seemed a world all its own. Immigrants from the Luther lands filled every region of the city and were known to its officials to be "thrifty, frugal, industrious, and productive."[6] Most of these newcomers were Lutheran rather than German Catholic and few of the Lutherans were of Scandinavian descent. As a peaceful, thriving culture, these children of the Reformation looked after growing families, maintained some land, and, by their sheer numbers, influenced the politics and development of the area.[7]

Born into this safe haven of German-Lutheranism, Anna learned the music of her heritage from the cradle on. Many years before, across the ocean, her maternal grandmother (the daughter of a church schoolmaster and a bell-ringer) had read Scripture to visiting pastors at the age of ten and memorized hymns. These texts strengthened and sustained her faith when both her parents passed away when she was twelve and later, when her own husband died when she was thirty-two.

This love of the chorale was passed down to her daughter, Emilie (Anna's mother), who memorized the same music to sing in the field and at the spinning wheel. In marrying Albert Hoppe in 1880, their shared love of hymns would embrace every one of their future children.[8] Emilie and her new husband planted their new family in this Midwestern metropolis in 1882, within a year of the birth of their first child, Otto. Following him, they brought into the world a total of nine children—Helen (1884), Earnest (1885), the future hymnwriter Anna (1889), and Arthur (1893). Four additional siblings passed away in infancy.[9]

For the greater part of Anna's life, the family lived together in Milwaukee. Anna writes how:

> The household tasks were performed to the tune of some Lutheran chorale, and when father came home at night, and we had the evening devotions, the old lamp would be out, but the singing continued as we knew the songs by heart. I still can picture our group singing by the light of the glowing embers of the old coal stove. "Come follow me, the Saviour spake" was my father's favorite. It is the song of the Christian warrior. He also reveled in a German rendition of the 91st Psalm, and I can hear him singing it yet.[10]

The young Hoppe siblings acclimated themselves well to music, including hymns from home instruction in their daily diversions. Anna relates further:

> There were five children, and at times a favorite pastime would be for one of us to hum a tune and the others guess the name of the hymn. The one who guessed it would then hum one, and so on. As the German treasury of Lutheran song is practically inexhaustible, we could spend hours that way. All of us were musically inclined, especially the boys, but we had not the means to procure an instrument nor to take lessons, but a little toy piano rendered splendid service and we all played the old melodies "by ear."[11]

With Albert's death in 1910, the financial wherewithal of the family plummeted, likely prompting the brothers to move away and start independent working careers. As early as 1900, Otto (the oldest) resided with his paternal aunt Minnie Jacob's family, along with his paternal grandfather Johann Hoppe, uncle August and cousin Gustav. By 1920 Minnie remarried and continued to board both Otto and August, along with their six daughters and two sons.[12] Anna, then twenty-one years old, soon sought employment at a local office as a "typewriter" or secretary to help support her family. There is a possibility that Anna's brothers may have enlisted in the

U. S. Army during World War I, but there are no extant records. Close to 1910, Earnest still resided at home, employed as a plumber. Records of his career and connection to the family drift away over the following decade.[13] Arthur married Hedwig Weinreich in Marion County, Indiana in 1916, and remained there for the rest of his life.[14] However, like her younger sister, Helen never left the home, but remained with her aging mother. Though Helen worked until at least the 1930s as a housekeeper, by the next decade her younger sister Anna was the sole supporter of the estate.[15] Of the five siblings, she appears to be the only one to attend and complete elementary school.

During these periods of family instability, hymns comforted Anna. She writes, "The old melodies brought me comfort and encouragement and cheer when death and sickness and trials and afflictions visited the little home, when we lost the homestead and things 'went black,' so to speak."[16] Of course, dark days occur in the stories of other hymnwriters. Like Anna, they were reminded that "whom the Lord loves, he chastens" (Hebrews 12:6). They embraced their cross as the revelation of God's goodness, which often stirred in them a "new song."

With this reshaping of the Hoppe home, prompted by the men's departure, the remaining mother and daughters took up residence in several places in Milwaukee during Anna's lifetime. As noted later, about 1917, she is reported to have lived at 2024½ Cherry Street. In 1928, she lived with her mother and sister at 2003 West Galena Street, at its intersection with North 20th Street, and only one-and-a-half miles from St. John's. In 1931, her address is recorded at 2122C North 16th Street, but by 1940, the three women lived at 2123B of the same address.[17] For Anna, each one of these locations was a short walk to church—less than one mile—and a streetcar ride to one of her ever-changing workplaces downtown.

Career

The Christian's life is made up of many roles and Anna's unified vocation presented itself in a diversity of employments. In 1910, she spent the whole of the year on the payroll of an office as a "typewriter" or clerical worker. During the publication of her hymn collection, she held a similar position at the L.J. Mueller Furnace Company

Anna with her co-workers

at 197 Reed Street.[18] By 1930, she was a dictaphone operator at the Westinghouse Electric Company. Ernest Edwin Ryden also cites "evening classes" as part of her training.[19] They likely prepared her in technical skills as an office assistant and were not associated with any academic degree. Her literacy acquired through her life at home and at church readied her the most for her hymnic contributions.

Parochial Life at St. John's

Anna's primary pastor, John Bading, was born November 24, 1824 in Rixdorf, Prussia, training for the ministry in Berlin and at the Hermansburg Mission Seminary. Ordained at age 29, he was sent to America by the Evangelical Society of Langenberg, Barmen and Elberfeld, and soon attained U. S. citizenship. Following calls to Calumet, Michigan and both Theresa and Watertown, Wisconsin, he assumed the presidency of the German Evangelical Lutheran Synod of Wisconsin and Other States from 1860-1864. In 1867 he was reinstated again as president after travels to Europe as an agent for Northwestern University. In addition to those responsibilities, he served on the university's board of trustees, and most important-ly tended to the flock at St. John's Evangelical Lutheran Church, Milwaukee, where Anna was baptized and confirmed.[20] Influenced by his contemporary, C.F.W. Walther (the father of the LCMS), Bading is credited for leading the young Wisconsin Synod in a con-fessional direction, linking with the Missouri Synod in the Synodical Conference rather than with the General Synod.[21]

St. John's Evangelical Lutheran Church, where Anna and her family worshipped and attended day school, was the site for two historical moments in American Lutheranism: the "marriage" of the Illinois, Minnesota, Missouri, Norwegian, Ohio, and Wisconsin Synods into the Synodical Conference in 1872, and also the formation of the Joint Evangelical Lutheran Synod of Wisconsin, Minnesota, Michigan, and other States in 1892.[22] As was frequently the case among early confessional Lutherans, the congregation had started in 1847 with a group meeting in a home. They soon invited Pastor Heinrich Ludwig Dulitz (1820-1885) to preach. The next year, he briefly served a more liberal group but soon resigned, and St. John's was incorporated in order to entreat him to stay. However, while Dulitz held membership in the Missouri Synod, St. John's did not, and their request to join was denied on the basis of Trinity Lutheran (LCMS) being too near the present church location.

Though its founding services were conducted entirely in German, Bading introduced additional English services in 1908, and both continued up until past the 1930s.[23] In 1869, the choir became mixed rather than men-only, and a tradition of strong music continued. Anna may have participated in the *Frauenverein*, a women's society at the church also active at the regional level, later known as the Ladies' English Bible Class. It also appears that St. John's supported several mission societies, for Anna later remarks that she attends "Jewish mission meetings, and the like." She also fostered an interest in home outreach, as seen later.

Anna, as an adult, reflected on her rich education at both the church and day school:

> St. John's Evangelical Lutheran church of the Wisconsin Synod, of which mother has been a member since she came to America back in 1881, maintained a Christian Day School, and does so still. Every class room had its own organ and had its own morning devotions. Our pastor, the sainted Rev. John Bading, had come from Hanover, Germany, and I remember how often he interspersed his sermons with the old hymn-words. His daughter Matilde was one of the teachers at the Christian Day School, and she taught the little ones their first Hosannas to the king,

and how those little ones could sing! The older children were instructed by Mr. Henry Behrens, who also hailed from Hanover, Germany, and had prepared for the ministry, but changed his mind and became a schoolmaster. And what a master he was in music and hymnody through the forty or more years he served the Church as teacher and choir-leader. Under his teaching we learned the old Lutheran chorales by heart and sang them to the tune of his violin and the class melodeon. In those days it was a common sight to see groups of children walking miles to the Christian School, reciting their catechism and hymns enroute, here in Milwaukee on the Lake.

Our teacher would tell us of the origin of the old hymns, and I never forgot the story he told us of George Neumark and his violin. In a time of depression he had to pawn his beloved treasure to get something to eat, and when he was able to redeem it, his overflowing heart burst forth in "Let, O my soul, thy God direct thee," number 484 in the *Augustana Hymnal*.[24]

Considering Anna's limited training, her vocabulary and writing skills are impressive, as is her understanding of Lutheran doctrine. Without a formal postsecondary education—still uncommon at her time—she understood the Christocentricity of Scripture, the division of Law and Gospel, the distinction between the work of the three Persons of the Trinity, and the union of Christ's two natures. Assuming that Pastor Bading oversaw her formative congregational life, under his care she became well-versed in doctrine through sermons, Bible classes, church activities, and Wisconsin Synod publications available there. Apparently, she also had access to Missouri Synod's books and articles. Later, it is evident that she admired the theology of Franz Pieper, Theodore Graebner, and William Dallmann (all LCMS theologians).[25] *The American Lutheran*, published by the Synodical Conference-sponsored American Lutheran Publicity Bureau, also was of aid, republishing some of her writing. Her mature poetic style reveals how thoroughly she knew other modern hymns, especially the poetry of Frances Havergal.

The fruits of Anna's informal education attest to the edification a single pastor and congregation can bestow on a member. If this experience of Christian education compelled a young woman like Anna to take up the hymnwriting pen, how much more will her faithful teachers be blessed and rewarded!

Relational Life

Coming of age as a German-Lutheran young woman in Milwaukee presented a special set of opportunities to Anna. With membership at the "capital" congregation of the Wisconsin Synod, she associated with synodical leaders regularly, including Pastor Bading at catechetical instruction. Completing the eighth grade at the church day school, she formed relationships with the other students along the way and gained respect as an active church member as she matured. The *Milwaukee Journal* of December 29, 1914 notes her serving as a bridesmaid for the wedding of two German-American friends.[26] Noticeably, her associates admired her, and social gatherings welcomed her company.

But, somewhere along the line, as Anna noted the married couples filling the sanctuary, it must have become apparent to her that she was not going to be married. For women of her socio-economic place in the early 20th century, this may not have been necessarily a disappointment at the lack of romantic interest, so much as a missed rite of passage. Young married women of later teenage years were automatically elevated to adult standing. Without a wedding ring and a home to manage, however, the young, single woman on her own would often be challenged by society to prove her adulthood.

Anna's remaining under the same roof as her mother and sister correlated to her educational level and single status. Dwelling alone while providing for her living needs would have proved difficult— and far more dangerous—then coexisting in the family home with the two other women. For health concerns or additional undocumented reasons, Emilie Hoppe (Anna's mother) may have required assistance around the home, and her daughters wished to stay with her of their own accord. Nevertheless, Anna's avid readership of Lutheran and American publications, inspiring her perseverance as a writer, would establish relationships beyond the walls of her modest house, her congregation, the desk in her downtown office, and the city limits of Milwaukee.

Anna's Life as a Hymnwriter (1914-1941)

Early Verse

Anna writes,

> I loved the dear old hymns, never dreaming that the time would come when God would grant me grace to write some myself...My first recollection of creative verse was a poem on Angels written for the autograph album of a class-mate, and I gave her three of them for good measure, instead of the one guardian poem allotted to childhood. In later years I penned another in honor of a lady teacher to whom I was, and am still, very much devoted. Then, in my early teens, I fell victim to hero worship, and "victimized" George Washington, and John Paul Jones, and Abraham Lincoln in verse, also the Battle of Gettysburg.[27]

Preceding her monumental number of submissions to *The Northwestern Lutheran*, young Anna practiced with "patriotic verse." On one occasion, she composed a poem in honor of a pastor martyred by the Knights of Columbus in February 1915. This Catholic brotherhood had resorted to committing acts of extremism against Protestants, of which this was a notable example.

In Memoriam

Dedicated to the memory of Rev. Wm. Black, slain by the Knights of Columbus at Marshall, Texas, in February 1915.

Ah, once again have Heaven's stately portals
Swung open wide 'midst strains of angels' song:
"Oh welcome to the Land of Blessed Immortals,
Thou martyred one and join the ransomed throng."

Another martyr's name on Hist'ry's pages,
Another voice is added to the song
Of martyred saints that echoes through the ages
In solemn strains, "How long, oh Lord, how long?"

Through Patmos' hallowed skies the song was swelling:
"Oh wilt Thou not avenge us, Lord, how long?"
And through the years the Book of Life is telling
Of Rome's black crimes, her unrepented wrong.

Oh Rome, thy doom is sealed in Revelations,
Thou dost not heed the Prophet's sore complaints,
Nor dost thou hear all Scripture's accusations,
For thou are drunken with the blood of saints.

But Heaven's record soon shall tell the story
Of countless saints thy cruel hand has slain.
Our martyred sire shall greet the King of Glory,
While floods of wrath on Babylon shall rain.

From earth's travail to Heaven's realm of glory,
Thy spirit, martyred one, has swiftly flown,
And in God's hallowed ground, serene and gory,
Thy fruitful martyr's blood was gently sown.

Thou art at rest, thy weary toil is ended,
Thy Savior's arms have fondly welcomed thee,
With other martyrs' blood thine own has blended.
We need not ask, "What will the harvest be?"

With eyes of faith we see thy Heav'nly glory,
Thy martyr's crown, thy robe of spotless white;
And here below thy name shall shine in story,
A beacon glow in Rome's so gloomy night.

Yea, thou art slain, but we are not repining,
Thy soul was filled with precious Gospel Light;
Whose rays of pristine beauty still are shining
Into the blackness of Rome's starless night.

We still await the glorious transition,
And follow thee in paths the saints have trod;
Soon we shall share thy joy in realms elysian,
Hallelujah! Amen! Glory be to God!

Anna Dorothy Hoppe, Milwaukee, Wis.[28]

Even in this example, her descriptive voice slowly emerges. Another such article, no publication source given, has surfaced:

Not Earthly Glory

(Dedicated to Evangelist and Ex-Romanist, L. J. King, of Toledo)

Oh man of God, thou seekest not earthly glory,
Thou dost not crave earth's dying wealth and fame,
Desirest not a hero's praise in story,
Nor dost thou seek to win a titled name.
Earth's passing glory settest thou at naught,
Yet has thou vict'ries won, and battle fought.

No silken badge, no medals gold adorn thee,
No earthly laurels crown thy burdened life,
And still, though cruel weapons oft have torn thee,
Hast thou emerged a victor through the strife.
Yet wieldest thou no earthly tyrant's sword,
Thy mighty armor is—"THUS SAITH THE LORD."

Thou hast not merely stood 'neath earthly banner,
In bold defense of honor and of law,
But thou hast fought in a triumphant manner
The scarlet monster John at Patmos saw.
Thy laurels are no earthly jewels bright,
But grateful hearts from darkness brought to light.

Like Paul of old, imprisoned, scourged,
Tortured and slandered, silenced, all but slain,
Yet while the harlot's hosts at feasts have eaten,
Rejoicing at thy fate, 'twas all in vain!
The Lord who guided Israel o'er the sea
Has still kept watch, my Christian friend, o'er thee.

No prison-bars, no pain, no desolation,
No slandering tongues, no fiendish craft sufficed
To cast thee from the Rock of thy salvation,
To tear thee from the Gospel of thy Christ.
Oh, battle on! Thy Jesus leads the way,
Thou Gideon, thou Luther of today!

'Tis all in vain Rome's mighty hordes pursue thee
'Tis all in vain they throw a thousand darts;
Oh, tremble not, her hosts cannot subdue thee,
Ten thousand prayers arise from loving hearts,
"Lord God of Hosts, whose name and power we sing,
Oh keep Thy servant 'neath Thy shelt'ring wing."

But Oh! the battle will not rage forever,
Soon will the brilliant morn of glory dawn;
Naught, naught can then from thy reward thee sever,
And, all thy trials will be past and gone,
When all earth's wickedness away is cast,
And Babylon has met her doom at last.

May God remain thy Strength and thy Defender,
May He bless thee and thine through all the years;
Blessed be thy home! and may the bounteous Sender
Of Heaven's gifts dry all thy bitter tears,
Until thou seest thy Saviour face to face,
Saved by His precious blood and glorious grace.

Composed by Miss Anna Hoppe,
Milwaukee, Wis.[29]

Yet, this bout of obsession soon gave way to more writings of a Christian theme. Anna continues, "After I left school, my literary tastes changed to spiritual literature, especially books of a prophetic nature."[30]

Beginnings in The Northwestern Lutheran

Moving towards a nationwide usage of English, the Wisconsin Synod's German *Quartalschrift* became known as the English *Northwestern Lutheran* in 1914, nearing Anna's twenty-fifth birthday. The first hymns springing from the English edition cite no source, but their nature and language suggest her authorship. However, this leaves unsettled why *The Northwestern Lutheran* chose to withhold her name.

During that summer, the day when the *Northwestern Lutheran* staff received a manuscript entitled "Saved by Grace" from Miss Anna Hoppe of Milwaukee, Wisconsin, the right eyes read the letter, welcoming it into the August 7 issue, and noting its return address. A St. John's member involved in the new magazine may have forwarded it, with or without Anna's sanction, or perhaps she accepted a commission. Whatever the case, her poems claimed an honored place in the periodical's office, and undoubtedly became a staple on the editor's desk for the upcoming quarter-century.

Opinion Essays

As if the regular inclusion of her hymns was not substantial enough, it appears that Anna often enclosed persuasive articles along with them, in addition to writing to local secular publications. Occasionally, *The Northwestern Lutheran* published opinion columns without giving the author's full name, or any at all. The same was the case with the inclusion of original poetry—it may be that Anna contributed to the publication more frequently than ascribed. These instances are rare, however, and the editors note her name often. Several articles are marked only "A.H.", as was customary, but her authorship is probable. If so, they reveal her personal adherence to confessional beliefs, as well as her audacious manner. Even in historical and apologetic works, her captivating literary style hinted at her forthcoming poetic writing.

One of these writings, released October 7, 1916, betrays this cover with Anna's clear tone, blending her knowledge of German-Lutheran history with an entreaty toward evangelism.

October 31

Ps 40:1-4

"I waited patiently for the Lord; and he inclined unto me, and heard my cry,

He brought me up also out of a horrible pit, out of the miry clay, and set my feet upon a rock and established my goings.

And he hath put a new song in my mouth, even praise unto our God; many shall see in and fear and shall trust in the Lord.

Blessed is that man that maketh the Lord his trust, and respecteth not the proud, nor such as turn aside to lies."

Truly, our Lutheran Church has every reason to say a hearty Amen to the inspired words of the Psalmist, for has not the Lord "inclined His ear and heard her cry?" Not only did He take Luther out of the "horrible pit" of Romanism, and out of the "miry clay" of papal darkness and superstition, placing his feet upon the solid, immovable Rock of His infallible word, but He has firmly established the Church which bears the name of the great reformer upon that Rock. He has put many a "new song" into her mouth—yes, she is known as the "Singing Church" and well deserves the title. She is "blessed," indeed in her firm trust in the Lord, and respects not the spiritual authority of proud Popery, nor "lends her ear to false doctrines, or to false prophets who turn aside to lies." October 31, 1917, will mark the 400th Anniversary of the Reformation. 'Neath the banner of "The Just shall live by Faith" our Lutheran Church has marched on through persecution, martyrdom, and conflict, and today, seventy-six million Lutherans in the world over are still singing "A mighty Fortress is our God," for "the kingdom has still remained ours."

The preparations which are in progress on a grand scale to make the 1917 Jubilee a success are meet and proper. Even the political world owes an enormous debt of gratitude to the Lutheran Reformation, as its principles are the source of the civil and religious liberty we now enjoy, as well as our liberal system of education. But the "cream" of the Lutheran Reformation is the restoration to the Church of the pure Gospel of Christ, and an open Bible. Self-evidently all Lutherans expect to join with hearts and voices in that grand jubilee, to sing the praises of Him who brought us out of darkness into His marvelous light. But—should we keep all our gratitude in cold storage until Oct. 31, 1917? The season of Mission Festivals is upon us, why not show our gratitude to the Lord now by doing all in our power to spread the Gospel for the restoration of which we claim to be so thankful?

The European War might prove a handicap to Foreign Missions, but we have Missions among the Indians and Negroes in our own land, and what about our Lutheran institutions? Besides, do we not owe an additional gratitude to the Lord for keeping our beloved country from the ravages of war, and allowing our church work to flourish unhampered? May He awaken in us the real missionary spirit and missionary consecration.

A heathen child, living in darkest Africa, who had known the Lord Jesus as her Savior but a short time, was asked by a missionary, together with other children, to give an offering to the Lord. Shortly after, she appeared with a great handkerchief full of coins amounting to so great a sum that the missionary exclaimed "My child, this is too much; where did you get this sum of money?" She smiled and said "Ah, sir, it is great joy to me to give this for what Jesus has done for me and what He is in my life. You taught me that He not only died for me, but lived for me every day He was on earth, pouring out His life for lost sinners, and I have been longing to do something for Him that would mean as much on my part, so I went to the planter and asked him how much he would give me if I would sell to him my life and be his slave, and he offered me all this money. The contract was signed, and I gave my life to work for him every day. So I hand you this, the price of my life, which I have brought to my precious Savior."

Little wonder that the missionary was overwhelmed at the sacrifice. But what are we giving the Lord as an offering of gratitude, we who have been brought up and reared in the Church of the Pure Word?

Our "*Gemeinde-blatt*" < parish newsletter> some time ago related an incident of an old German, who contributed his share toward a certain fund far in advance of the time required, and when his pastor inquired the reason he replied:

"Des Herrn Werk muss getan werden, ich
kann ja sterben." *[The work of the Lord must
get done, then I can truly die.]*

This seems to be capital advice for all who would fain
keep their prospective tokens of gratitude in storage
until October 1917. That date is likely to find us members of the triumphant "Singing Church" in glory. The
Church does not ask a sacrifice as great as that of the
little African maiden, but ought we not be willing to
place a worthy offering on the altar as a token of love
and gratitude to Him who gave every drop of His life for
us, and who is now preparing a place for us in glory? By
the way, have all our gifts for missionary purposes really
been "sacrifices"?

"He took me out of the miry clay,
He set my feet on the Rock to stay,
He puts a song in my soul today
A song of praise, Hallelujah."

All this He has done for us, as Lutherans. What are we
doing for Him? A.H.[31]

The *Milwaukee Journal* issued on October 13, 1917 published
a fiery editorial by Anna, defending local German-Lutheran clergy
who had refused to promote from their pulpits certain civic food
conservation programs. It appears that the pastors had been singled
out for criticism based on their ethnicity rather than creed. Anna
promptly corrected the editors:

Defends Pastor for Not Aiding Food Plan

"Under the caption 'Won't Preach Saving of Food from
Pulpit', the Oct. 11 issue of *The Journal* mentioned the
refusal of certain Lutheran pastors, 'of German names'
in Milwaukee to use their pulpits as platforms for lectures on food conservation," writes Anna Hoppe, 2024½
Cherry St., to *The Journal*. Defending the attitude of these
pastors, she continues:

"I would like to ask why pastors of 'German names' were selected. Is it because of the undisputed fact that the Germans excel in the art of cookery? Whatever may have been the purpose of the request, I beg to disagree with you if in your opinion their refusal indicated a lack of patriotism. Love of country and true patriotism are imbedded in the great confessions of the Lutheran church, and if you would enter the churches presided over by these pastors, you would hear the most fervent prayers ascend to God for preservation of our country, for divine governance of those holding the reins of government, as well as for the welfare of its inhabitants. Anyone acquainted with history knows that patriotism is Lutheranism's 'second name.' It was so in the days of the immortal Muhlenberg and is so still. The thousands of Lutheran young men in the service of our country at this time are proof of this.

"The reason these pastors refused to preach on food conservation is because it is not the mission of the church. The church is a divine institution, organized by Christ for the propagation of the gospel, and for the preaching of the pure word of God, the priceless possession of which we Lutherans expect to commemorate in our Quadri-Centennial jubilee this year. Our constitution advocates the complete separation of church and state which is in entire harmony with Lutheran doctrine. The state does not desire the interference of the church in its affairs, and rightly so, but, to be candid, are the state's representatives not dangerously close to meddling with church affairs, when they desire to dictate what our pastors should preach? Pastors have been asked to preach about Liberty bonds, they've been requested to act as recruiting agents for the government by encouraging the young men in their congregations to enlist, and now comes food conservation, for which topic pastors bearing 'German names' are supposedly best fitted.

"These things are all well and good, if our pastors wish to make it a 'side issue,' but the Lutheran pulpit is no place for discussions of this sort. Much has been said about 'the power of the press'; why not leave it to the press and public lecturers to expound food conservation.

"Sad to state, many so-called Christian churches in the land today have missed their calling, turning their pulpits into lecture platforms where every topic except the gospel comes up for discussion, and what is the result? 'Ichabod' (God has departed) is written over the door. These churches might be excellent social and philanthropic organizations, but they are not evangelical churches.

"It is my earnest prayer that the Lutheran church continue to preach the word, the disregard of which in these perilous times threatens to bring to fulfillment the prophecy, 'Behold, I will send a famine in the land, not a famine of bread, nor a thirst for water, but of hearing the word of the Lord.'

"If the churches remain true to their trust in 'seeking first the kingdom of God,' then He who fed the 5,000 with a few loaves and fishes will also take charge of the food conservation in our beloved country.

"By supplying chaplains, testaments, religious literature, etc., to the boys in the army and navy [sic], by prayers for the country's welfare, and strict adherence to its divinely appointed mission of preaching the gospel, the church, in calling sinners to repentance, renders the country a greater service than by turning its sacred pulpits into lecture platforms for the discussion of subjects like the above mentioned.

"An article in *The Presbyterian of the South* under the caption of "Church and the Government", also voices its disapproval of requests of this sort made to pastors."[32]

In this instance, Anna's theological education shines forth, foreshadowing the urgent, Scriptural tone of her hymnody. First of all, she recognizes that the missions of the temporal and heavenly kingdoms must not be mixed, lest each interpose upon the other against God's will. Additionally, she affirms that the Gospel demands precedence in every sermon, as the center around which each work of the Christian life is an aspect. Without it, faith becomes a religion of works. She also believes slighting this Word will produce a dry spell from the Gospel rain. Failing to reap the harvest of true preaching year after year does not merit another season of grace, if people so resolve that they have plenty.

Along with the poem "Build Thou the Walls of Zion," Anna encouraged Lutherans to nurture their little ones through home, school, and mission instruction, inspired by an orphanage confirmation service.

"Feed My Lambs"

It is a pleasant experience to be present in a Lutheran home, where family worship has not become a "lost art," and witness the little ones climb on mother's knee, lifting their childish heart and voices in prayer to Him who delights to hear His praises "from out of the mouths of babes." Thanks be to God, we still have mothers who have not ignored the admonition of Christ to "feed the lambs" placed in His arms at Holy Baptism, mothers whose cherished hope it is to have the little ones enrolled in a Lutheran Parochial and Sunday School, where they may continue to be nourished with "the milk of the Word," increase in Wisdom, and grow in grace. Parents who rear their children in the fear of the Lord have every reason to rejoice, when at confirmation these children renew their baptismal vows, and pledge unswerving loyalty to Christ, His Word, and His Church.

Our Lutheran Church also heeds the words of its divine Master— "Feed my Sheep," — in preaching the pure gospel in its pulpits, maintaining Bible Classes, and higher institutions of learning, where the lambs it has reared in childhood, may continue to thrive and grow "unto the measure of the stature of the fullness of Christ." God bless our Lutheran institutions, grant us warm hearts and open hands to support them, and give us more homes where family worship is not a "lost art." Much of the loyalty of the confirmed to the Church depends upon the environment of the home.

It is not the purpose of this article to chide such Lutherans as fail to take advantage of all the blessings to which the Church of the Reformation is heir, but to contrast their privileges with those of others among us who are less fortunate. Are there not "other sheep" who have not had the advantages of a Lutheran home, a Lutheran Parochial and Sunday School, a Lutheran Church, who have perhaps never heard of the Savior? Yes, many of them, and the Lord has graciously opened the door to the missionary endeavors of our Lutheran Church, not only in the foreign field, and among the Indians and Negroes, but he has also given us the opportunity to seek and save the lost in the confines of our State Institutions. For year our Synodical Conference has conducted mission-stations at these institutions, and, according to the last report of our busy City Missionary, the Rev. Enno Duemling, 15,000 inmates had the Gospel preached to them during the past year. It was the privilege of the writer to attend the confirmation exercises of a class of catechumens, numbering 21, at the Milwaukee County Home for Dependent Children Sunday, Sept. 23rd. Prior to confirmation, our missionary administered Holy Baptism to several members of the class.

The scholars of the Lutheran Sunday School, numbering about one hundred, were present at the service. The Sunday School is in the charge of Mr. Jos. A Klug, whose long experience as a Lutheran School teacher renders him very efficient. A student at our Wauwatosa seminary, Mr. Richard Janke, also renders assistance. Through the kindness of the County Board, and the Superintendent these children are permitted to receive instruction in the Catechism, Bible History, and are taught the beautiful songs of our Lutheran Hymnal, the Creed, Lord's Prayer, Psalms, and other prayers.

When the Lord says "Let the little ones come unto me" these orphaned, neglected children, and such whose parents are ill or in prison, are surely included, many of them coming from homes where prayer and the Bible are unknown. The seed sown in this institution through regular instruction is sure to yield abundant fruitage.

What attracts a stranger instantly is the attachment of the children to their teachers and our missionary. They are very attentive, and anxious to learn.

It was inspiring to hear the Confirmation Class renew their baptismal vows and promise loyalty to Christ and His Church until death. And the singing! Never did the words of the beautiful hymn, "Jesus, Be Our Guide" strike home to the writer with more force than when these children sang them, each line seeming as though penned for them especially:

> "When the world is cold, let us to Thee hold,
> When the cup of sorrow draining,
> We may do so uncomplaining,
> For through trials we find our way to Thee."

> "When affliction's smart, anguishes the heart,
> Though our life be woe and weakness
> Help us bear the cross in meekness,
> May we bear in mind God's a Father kind."

It seems indeed that the world has been cold to them, that they have had a cup of sorrow to drain, a life of affliction and anguish of heart, a cross to bear, still their faith enabled them to continue:

> "Order Thou our ways, Lord, through all our days,
> Though our path be dark and cheerless,
> Jesus with us, we'll be fearless,
> Open when life's o'er, Lord to us Thy door."

May the Lord abundantly bless the toil of our missionary for the salvation of immortal souls. May he grant that these children are placed in Lutheran homes, to become useful members of our Church, and may we all continue in prayer for our missionary, showing our gratitude and Christian love by diligently supporting the blessed work by means of which others are converted to the Gospel, and led to walk in the path of life in which we ourselves are walking by divine grace. May He establish the work of our hands and give us willing hearts to contribute to the cause of missions, remembering the promise that "they who turn many to righteousness shall shine as the stars forever and ever." Anna Hoppe.[33]

The quality and availability of parochial schools remained an issue under contention. Growing up in one and witnessing its continued activity day by day, Anna adeptly supported their sustenance. Peppered with a rightful indignation, she spreads out the case for private Lutheran instruction to the local newspaper.

A Defense of the Lutheran Parochial School
(By one of its "products".)

If the *Milwaukee Journal* of Sunday, January 13th, reported correctly, a German Baptist pastor of this city paid the following "compliment" to our Lutheran Church Schools: "I absolutely disapprove of the parochial school, where the point of view and the language of the old country is kept up, and the children 'do not learn to think in American terms.' In the same article, the Pastor of an Evangelical Church has this "tribute" to pay: "Our Church has never believed in the parochial school, 'because we wanted the children to become thoroughly Americanized in the Public School.'"

In other words, these pastors apparently wish to have it understood that in their opinion our Lutheran Parochial Schools are un-American, and consequently not patriotic. Can these reverend gentlemen vouchsafe for the truth of this statement? Have they any convincing proofs?

Since the entry of the United States in the war against Germany, numerous articles have appeared in the secular press of the country questioning the patriotism and loyalty of Lutherans of German descent, merely because that denomination had its birth in a German University, and because the cradle of the Lutheran Reformation happened to stand on German soil. These articles, which fairly flooded our newspapers and magazines, received convincing refutation and rebuke from the pens of our pastors and laymen with the result that the secular press recently proclaimed in broad headlines: "Lutherans are loyal!"

But why should Protestant pastors who know and teach the Word of God to their flocks: "Bring up your children in the nurture and admonition of the Lord" have any objection to the Lutheran Church for doing so? These pastors know that our Lutheran Parochial Schools lay great stress on the teaching of the Scriptures, in obedience to Divine command. Therefore, from a Christian standpoint our schools need no earthly defense for their existence. The Bible defends them. These clerical critics also know that a large percentage of our parochial schools have been placed on the "accredited list" by our Public-School Superintendents, which indicates that their standard in secular branches, English included, is equivalent to that set by the Public Schools, and, in consequence, the graduates of these Lutheran schools are admitted to the Public High School without further preparation or examination.

But what about the Patriotism in the Lutheran Schools?

For the information of these pastors the writer would state that in this respect our Lutheran Schools stand "head and shoulders" over the Public Schools, because they teach, proclaim, and instill into the minds and hearts of their charges a patriotism of so exalted a type as to be impossible for an institution to reach, which has not the Bible. Because our Lutheran Schools teach the Bible, they are the very bulwark of the nation. The children are taught to "render unto Caesar the things that are Caesar's". They are taught to be "subject to the higher powers" because they are ordained by God. They are taught to pray for their government, because the Bible enjoins that "first of all, supplications, intercessions, and giving of thanks be made for all men; for kings, and for all that are in authority, that we may lead a quiet and acceptable life in all godliness and honesty. For this is good and acceptable in the sight of God and our Savior."

Our Lutheran Church has heeded the command of the Lord with regard to the rearing of its children, and in doing so, has reaped a bountiful harvest, which proves beyond doubt, that the Lord's blessing is upon those who heed the inspired admonition of Paul to Timothy. Since Bible Truth constitutes the very warp and woof of teaching in the Lutheran Schools, its scholars, as Christians, must be patriotic, and the Lord be praised, history shows that they have been, experience proves that they are! The Missouri Synod alone has 50,000 boys with the colors, and in all, nearly 200,000 Lutherans have joined the American Army or Navy in the present conflict, a large percentage of whom are parochial school graduates. Since it is evident that our Lutheran parochial schools equal the Public Schools in secular branches, and are above them as far as true Christian Patriotism is concerned, is the teaching of German a reflection on their Americanism, as these pastors seem to insinuate? Far from it! Thousands of German-American Lutherans spilled their life-blood in the Civil War, when all had to admit that Lutheran patriotism stood the test. Still our Lutheran Schools were not founded for the purpose of maintaining the German language, but for rooting and grounding the children entrusted to their care in the infallible Word of the Lord, which alone can make them "wise unto salvation", and wise also in their attitude in matters of secular education and patriotism.

As the pastors above referred to apparently consider our Lutheran Schools un-American because they tolerate the German language, the following words by Prof. Graebner of St. Louis, published in *The Lutheran Witness* in answer to an article in *Everybody's Magazine*, questioning the loyalty of Wisconsin Lutherans of German descent, are very masterly and to the point: "Never have our Parochial Schools been a vehicle of German *Kultur*. Their purpose has been these seventy-five years to rear Christian Citizens of the United States, and faithful Church members. Not even in the language-classes have any text-books been employed that were printed or written in Germany. Never has the history of Germany been taught in our parochial schools. The virtues inculcated were not specifically German, but 'Christian' virtues. These virtues the scholars took into business and into political life, and by their thrift, honesty, and piety have helped to make the United States the nation that she is today. Our parochial schools have, with the exception of religious instruction and its linguistic basis, been thoroughly Americanized, even in language. Many have dropped the German language entirely. These schools have never been used as a vehicle of the 'Deutschland über alles' spirit, but of the 'Christian Education above all' spirit. It was not the parochial school, not even the language, but simply and purely racial origin which caused German-Americans of all and of no religious affiliations to support the efforts looking to the maintenance of peaceful relations with Germany before war was declared. To taunt the Lutheran Church with an "un-American spirit" because German is maintained as the language of worship and is still taught as a branch in our schools, is a procedure which places an undeserved stigma upon millions of loyal American citizens." So far Prof. Graebner.

The writer is convinced that ten thousands of Wisconsin Lutherans could testify that the Christian environment they obtained in the Lutheran parochial schools gave them as exalted a view of American principles and true patriotism as it is possible for an educational institution to present. The "Christian Herald" of January 26, 1914, was right when it stated in an article pertaining to the religious training of children: "The Lutherans have many parochial schools and these are like spiritual oases in the great desert of American childhood."

Would to God we had more of these oases, where our children receive the Bread and Water of Life daily in the pleasant pastures of God's Holy Word. They find out soon enough that the world without has only husks to offer, cares naught for their spiritual welfare, and "what does it profit a man if he gain the whole world and lose his own soul"? God bless our Lutheran parochial schools, these bulwarks of Christian life, Christian citizenship, Christian patriotism, these staunch advocates of the greatest of American principles, the separation of Church and state, these defenders of the Bible against the onslaughts of Higher Criticism, Evolution, New Thought, Infidelity, and the countless false doctrines and Isms of the day, which lay their traps to ensnare and beguile the Church's treasures, its children. The Lord bless and prosper them is the prayer of "a grateful product."

ANNA HOPPE.

To Our Parochial Schools

Dear Lutheran Schools, long, long may ye flourish,
Long, long may ye prosper, thrive and expand;
Long may your teachers continue to nourish
With the Bread of Life the babes of the land.
O be not mindful of earth's hollow shams,
The Master commandeth you: "Feed my Lambs."

Heed not the glitter of worldly-wise learning,
Nor the rantings and taunts of Godless fools,
For the Water of Life our youth is yearning,
It flows in your midst, dear Lutheran Schools.
O keep it flowing! Continue to reap
The blessings of Him who said: "Feed my Sheep."

"Seek first the kingdom," the Master commandeth,
Dear Lutheran Schools, to your trust be true!
Firm as a Rock the Savior's promise standeth:
"All things then shall then be added unto you".
How hallowed your precincts where Jesus rules!
Be loyal to Him, dear Lutheran Schools.

God bless you, dear Schools, God make you a blessing
To childhood, to youth, to the young and old.
May the pure Gospel you now are confessing
Lead countless thousands to the Gates of Gold.
God bless you dear Schools, in every land;
May you grow and prosper, thrive and expand.

ANNA HOPPE,
January 15th, 1918.
Milwaukee, Wis. [34]

Those in society, not distinguishing between church and state, may have wished the parochial schools to advocate for social responsibility, partly by furthering the use of English. Yet, Lutheran pastors concentrated on preserving German for practicality. At this point, the best confessional literature issued from their native land, and both translating and reprinting in America would be expensive and tedious. August Pieper's cry—"I want to be saved in German!"[35]— reflected the outcome of this situation, not the premise. Anna and many other Wisconsin Synod Lutherans may have disputed the idea.

Another article entitled "Is the Gospel of the First Century Too Old-Fashioned for the Twentieth?" appeared in *The Northwestern Lutheran* on April 21, 1918. Upon reading an article in a women's magazine that encouraged postmodern preaching, Anna felt charged to enlighten her Wisconsin Synod audience on current issues. Here, she also names the Lutheran Church as the solution the author overlooked. In this essay, one observes her conservative critical thinking prefiguring her poetic themes.

The *Ladies' Home Journal* of March 1918, contains a lengthy article from the pen of the Rev. Joseph H. Odell, D.D., entitled "Why I Cannot Preach My Old Sermons

Now." The editor of the periodical mentioned adds this comment: "there is not a preacher in America but should carefully read, ponder over, and personally apply the message that is written strong and direct in this article. The pew already feels it but is beginning to wonder whether the pulpit realizes it."

In order to give the readers of *The Northwestern Lutheran* who perchance have not read the article mentioned, but who have "already felt the message which every preacher in America should carefully read, ponder over, and personally apply" an opportunity to ascertain whether their respective pastors have "fully realized it", the following excerpts from the Rev. Odell's "message" are quoted:

"My experience," said a ministerial friend, "teaches me that people do not want the preacher to touch upon current events of contemporaneous history in his sermons. For one thing, they think they know more about such matters than he does, and for another, they object to a secularization of the pulpit. The overwhelming majority wants just the plain old Gospel, delivered with traditional dignity".

"Shades of the Prophets! Think upon it!

"If Moses, or Isaiah, or Jeremiah, or Ezekiel, or Christ, or Paul, or Peter or John happened to be living today, he would not be available for a modern sacrosanct pulpit.

"If St. Augustine, or Savonarola, or Wycliffe, or St. Francis of Assisi, or Calvin, or Knox, or Wesley should be in our midst, he could not receive a call to the pastorate.

"If Edwards, Finney, Bushnell, Beecher, Storrs or Phillips Brooks was now here and in his prime, not a church would desire him.

"If my ministerial friend was correct, then not a man who had part or lot in making the Bible would be eligible as a public servant of God today. Indeed, when I come to think of it, if that canon had been applied to preachers in the past we should never have had a Bible at all.

"There is another reason also, why I think the statement far from true. The overwhelming majority of people on Sunday morning are playing golf or tennis, sailing or automobiling, sleeping or reading the newspaper, and seem to prefer such occupations to the stirring up of the ancient doctrinal dust which passes as "just the plain old Gospel." They treat the church as an archaic remnant of another age, a dull survival of the immemorial past, a thing irrelevant to modern life. Why? Not because they do not need light and guidance, and inspiration, but because they do not find such help in the church for life as they have to live it today. Living amid the grueling realities of the twentieth century, they are impatient of truth which can express itself only in terms of the first, fifth, or the fifteenth century."

"They do not care a snap of their fingers whether Abraham was justified by faith or works, if predestination can be reconciled with free will, how many Isaiahs wrote the book which bears that name, when and how the world will end. All they want is a spiritual interpretation of the world-rending and home-smashing events that are taking place. Everything else can wait."

The Rev. "Doctor of Divinity" continues:

"It so happens that I am the blessed or accursed possessor of a sermonic "barrel". Three hundred sermons, fully written, tempts me week by week. Three hundred sermons! Three hundred sermons cold and dead. Yes, so dead that I dare not even hope for a resurrection. They can no more be preached again than the men can fight who passed away at Gallipoli or on the fields of Flanders. The war killed the sermons just as the war slew the men."

"One can preach often upon sacrifice, self-abnegation, self-surrender, vicarious suffering, obedience to the will of God, reconciliation and atonement, without saying much. But who need falter now, with the blood-red glory of vicarious sacrifice dying hundreds over miles of French and Italian soil, and even staining afresh the sands of Palestine!

"The men of Liege, the valiant British force that was all but wiped out between Mons and Ypres, the unspeakably gallant French armies on the Marne and at Verdun, these lead us with unfaltering steps straight "to the place that is called Calvary." Men are still dying for men, for liberty, for honor, for truth, for righteousness. No-one need hesitate again to picture the splendid tragedy of Golgatha, where one could not save Himself and save others too, when the redeeming act is multiplying itself by the millions before our very eyes."

"Sermons on the social element in the Gospels expositions of Pauline theology, descriptive discourses upon the romantic incidents in the history of Israel, careful studies in the reconciliation of Science and religion, well, they all did good service in their day, but in matter and mood they would be considered an impertinence now."

We pause for breath and ask WHITHER IS MODERN PROTESTANTISM DRIFTING?

It certainly does seem strange that a "modern" Doctor of Divinity should be surprised when a ministerial friend (who probably was a bit old-fashioned), informs him of his experience that the majority of people who attend church want "just the plain old Gospel." The reverend Doctor also seems surprised at the apparent opinion of his friend that the exponents of "the ancient doctrinal dust" such as Knox, Wesley, Savonarola, Finney, and others would not be welcome in the pulpits of fashionable American Churches today. The sum and substance of the article indicates that in the opinion of its author the "plain old Gospel" as preached by the apostles to Christians in the first century does not satisfy the Christians of the twentieth, its "shortcoming" being especially noticeable in the case of those whose loved ones have left to "die for liberty, honor, truth, and righteousness."

The Scriptural "thinking themselves wise, they became fools" [Romans 1:22/Ed.] immediately suggests itself when articles such as the foregoing are given prominence in our secular magazines, and one's assurance is made doubly sure that the Reformed branch of Protestantism has to a great extent drifted from its moorings. Writers in various periodicals of Reformed denominations have repeatedly affirmed the fact when they claimed that a Calvin, Knox, Finney, and Wesley would be unwelcome in the pulpits of their respective churches today. Higher Criticism, Evolution, New Thought, and other Modernisms which have crept into Reformed colleges during the past century have caused a Munhall to cry out: "Breakers, Methodism Adrift!", a Spurgeon to utter his burning words in defense of evangelical truth against what he termed the "downgrade movement" in the Baptist church, which resulted in his resignation from the Baptist Union in 1887, and a Pierson to drop his name from the Presbyterian Church, because he no longer desired to be "unequally yoked together with unbelievers". Those who have read Haldemann's "Songs of the Times" must consider it as a miracle indeed that there is any primitive Christianity left in the Reformed branch of Protestantism. So great has been the apostasy from "the faith once delivered to the saints" and so outspoken their criticisms of the Bible, that an evangelical missionary who for the same reason withdrew from the Congregational communion recently suggested that their respective seminaries hang out a sign "Heresy Hunters Not Wanted", so as to leave them undisturbed in their settled unbelief. Hundreds in pulpit and pew, however, have heeded the call of the Bible and conscience. "Come out from among them and be ye separate."

But can it be possible that the Rev. Odell is correct when he states that Protestant laymen are indifferent as to the doctrine of Justification? If it is true that they do not care "a finger snap" about the very foundation truth of Protestantism, why do they not return to the Law entirely, join the Jewish synagogue, or the Church of Rome? Undoubtedly, there are thousands of modern "Athenians" in our day who are continually seeking "some new thing", and their number appears to have increased considerably since the days of Paul. The "plain old Gospel" has ceased to give them what they crave for, so they much prefer a "modern" pastor, preferably a recent graduate of what Haldemann terms a "Jericho College," who will tickle their ears with lectures on all the issues of the day, from the latest in fashions to politics and the controversy between Capital and Labor.

The Rev. Odell appears to be one of the advocates of the popular doctrine that all who die in battle are saved eternally, whether they accept Christ as their Savior or not. He apparently considers their sacrifice a passport to heaven. But has this conception the sanction of the infallible "Thus saith the Lord"? Far from it. Acts 4, verse 12 makes this clear enough, as do numerous other passages of Scripture. True it is, the Scriptural statement: "Greater love hath no man that this, that a man lay down his life for his friends" [John 15:13/ Ed.] might well be applied to our boys on the battlefields of Europe, but what are all human sacrifices compared to the sacrifice of the Son of Man on Calvary? Even sectarian periodicals have called attention to the danger of this "salvation by works" theory.

Thank God, our beloved Lutheran Church still preaches the "plain old Gospel" of "Justification by Faith," of Salvation by Grace alone without the deeds of the Law. The war has not "killed" the sermons that appear on the printed pages of her literature, nor can it kill the verbal ones that echo from her pulpits today, for "the Word of the Lord endureth forever" [1 Peter 1:25/Ed.]. She has sent that Eternal Word to her thousands of boys who are with the colors, in the firm hope that "the plain old Gospel" alone can comfort and guide them, as its comforts and guides their loved ones at home. As far as considering Pauline theology an "impertinence" in this worldly-wise twentieth century, she continues to put her trust in the writing of that great apostle as the inspired Word of God. Grant God, that the Mother church of the Reformation will continue to defend that bulwark of Protestantism, "the Just shall live by Faith", as the Pearl of great Price, whether present day Pharisees "care a finger snap" about the doctrine or not. She might be old-fashioned, and woefully behind the times since she clings to "the ancient doctrinal dust", and faithful to her mission, still preaches "the plain old Gospel", but she has the Scriptural assurance: "Heaven and Earth shall pass away, but the Word of the Lord endureth forever". With this war-torn world on the verge of collapse, what better security or firmer foundation can she ask?

Now, having "carefully read, pondered over, and personally applied" Dr. Odell's wonderful "message", the writer of these lines is convinced that the "plain old Gospel" of the first century is just as up-to-date in the twentieth, and the Lord be praised, our Lutheran pastors have "always realized it." No, Mr. Odell, not all the "ladies" who read *The Ladies Home Journal* agree with you.

"Preserve Thy Holy Word, dear Lord,
Preserve it through the ages,
For worldly wisdom's carnal sword
With might against it rages,
Ever alert for something new,
A worldly pulpit, worldly pew,
Ignores its sacred pages.

Preserve Thy flock, O gracious Lord,
Forsake nor leave us never,
Bind us securely to Thy Word
That naught the bonds can sever.
Thy promise still remaineth sure,
That great Gibraltar shall endure
Forever and forever.

Anna Hoppe.[36]

"Is the Distribution of Tracts Worth While?" advocates the Reformed practice of evangelism for Lutherans, asserting it as a helpful tool rather than a self-promoting advertisement. This article, as others, originally appeared in *The Northwestern Lutheran;* then, having accrued attention, other Lutheran presses took up its printing.

Is the Distribution of Tracts Worth While?

Much has been said and written in Reformed circles regarding the advantages of and blessings following the systematic distribution of "Gospel Tracts." Christian workers in Reformed denominations have circulated them by the thousands, inserting them in their personal mail, passing them out on the streets, and making extensive use of them in missionary work. Mention is frequently made in Reformed periodicals of the zeal with which these tract-distributors, both clergy and laity, carry on their work of acquainting others with the Gospel, and large Tract Societies have been organized to perpetuate the work.

Shall we Lutherans, who possess the Word of God in its pristine purity and primitive beauty take a back seat, or stand idly by while Christian workers in other denominations are using these "silent preachers" as a means to bring souls to Christ?

There have been justified objections in Lutheran circles in regard to certain methods employed by tract-distributors to gain publicity, and an "audience" for their "silent preachers," but it cannot be denied that these tracts have accomplished wonders. One frequently hears of conversions due to the reading of one or more of these Gospel Tracts. The following narrative, which has frequently appeared in Reformed periodicals, will serve as an illustration:

"A tract, dropped in the way of Richard Baxter, was the means of his conversion. Richard Baxter wrote "The Call of the Unconverted" which led to the conversion of multitudes, among others Philip Doddridge. The latter wrote

"The Rise and Progress of Religion in the Soul," which is understood to have brought thousands in the kingdom, among others the great Wilberforce. Wilberforce wrote "A Practical View of Christianity," which was the means of bringing many to Christ, among others Leigh Richmond, who became the author of "The Dairyman's Daughter," through the reading of which many were brought to a knowledge of the Savior." Have we Lutherans no opportunity to acquaint others with the doctrines and practices of our beloved Lutheran Church by means of tracts? Yes, opportunity to do so is knocking at our doors very audibly just now, and it behooves us to become aware of the fact and "get busy."

During the Jubilee Year, the American Lutheran Publicity Bureau did a very commendable work in the publication of tracts acquainting those of other denominations or of no church affiliation with the teachings of our Church. Tracts entitled "What the Evangelical Lutheran Church Stands For," "Salvation," "The Bible Church," "Why Lutheran Parish Schools" and others have received the wide distribution and ready sale they well deserved, but should the circulation of these tracts cease now that the Jubilee Year is past? Indeed not. On the contrary, let us be more energetic than ever in their systematic distribution, and this can be done in a method sanctioned by, and in keeping with Lutheran principles.

In addition to the tracts issued by the American Lutheran Publicity Bureau, which can also be obtained through the Publishing Houses of our Synodical Conference, the tract series of which the Rev. William Dallmann is the author, have done admirable service in the past, and we ought to prove our love toward the Lutheran Church, and our appreciation of the author's work by doubling our efforts to give these tracts the wide circulation they merit. Words often fail us in giving bold and clear testimony to the unbeliever regarding the faith we hold so dear, and this is often the case when we are called upon to give an answer to those of other denominations. We are often asked why we are called Lutherans, why we differ from other Protestants on certain doctrines, why we object to the theatre, the dance, and the lodge, what our teaching is in regard to Sabbath observance, temperance, conversion, and baptism, why we believe the Bible to be the inspired Word of God, why we are in conflict with the Church of Rome, and why our doctrine of the Lord's Supper differs from that taught by the Reformed denominations. All these, and other vital subjects have been very masterly treated by the Rev. Dallmann, and published in tract form, not to occupy space, and serve as an ornament upon the shelves of our Publishing Houses, but for the purpose of being read and studied by us as Lutherans and circulated by the thousands among outsiders.

That the careful and prayerful distribution of these "silent preachers" may serve to enlighten the unbeliever, convince the skeptic, give those of other denomination an answer as to the faith that is in us, and that an earnest study of their contents may strengthen the Lutheranism of our laymen, is the prayer of the writer in wishing these tracts and booklets Godspeed in their heavenly mission of preaching the Gospel to every creature.

ANNA HOPPE.
in *The Northwestern Lutheran.*[37]

Upon the departure of a renowned atheistic, German professor, Anna seized the opportunity to reflect on the comfort true Christian faith bestows at life's end. Her personal studies of other worldviews and "Higher Criticism" here avail themselves to her fellow Lutherans.

Thoughts on the Death of Haeckel

Numerous comments and editorials upon the recent death, at Jena, Germany, of the distinguished naturalist, Ernst Heinrich Haeckel, have lately appeared in the secular press. One of the rather interesting comments was to the effect that it took the great professor of Zoology but a moment to ascertain the truth or non-truth of the immortality of the soul, which he so persistently denied during his career, the moment he crossed the great beyond, and the writer wondered whether the great naturalist would return and by means of spirit manifestation state the facts to some acknowledged authority engaged in psychical research.

While other brilliant authors of his type opposed to the Christ religion advanced the theory of the soul's immortality as a possibility at least, Haeckel boldly denied it. His "Origin and Genealogy of the Human Race" is even more extreme in its exposition of evolution than Darwin's "Origin of Species." While it is the impression in some circles that Darwin advanced his particular views as "theories" only, without any intention to deny the existence of a personal God, this cannot be said of Haeckel. A writer in a Missionary Paper some time ago stated that the great Darwin, shortly before his death, placed his hands upon the Bible, and exclaimed: "This Book only is the Truth. I advanced my opinions as theories only, but they spread like wild-fire, and many have placed a false construction upon them." Sad to state, numerous Reformed seminaries in our day not only fail to condemn this theory as antagonistic to the Scriptures, but in order to be modern, accept it, even interpreting the six days of Creation in Genesis as symbolical, so as to bolster up the opinion that the creation of the earth was an evolutionary process covering six thousand years at least. To give it further Scriptural sanction they have even gone so far as to quote the text "A thousand years in Thy sight are but as yesterday, and as a watch in the night" (Psalm 90:4). In quarters where the inspiration of Holy Scripture is denied, Darwinism has replaced the Creation story of Genesis, which has been called a "myth" not only in the classrooms of non-religious colleges, but even among the clergy of Reformed denominations.

But will the apparently fearless death of Haeckel strengthen the convictions of the agnostics, infidels, and skeptics? Have his tireless investigations brought them any nearer to the truth which they are ever seeking, and ever failing to find? *The Truth Seeker*, a free-thought and agnostic weekly published in New York City, contains an article in its August 16th issue entitled "How the great Renan died," of which the following is an extract: "he went through life, as one of humanity's greatest philosophers and teachers, meeting death at last with Socratic candor and courage, convinced of life's final dissolution into nothingness—the blessed Nirvana—leaving behind him his teachings as an immortal legacy." Commenting upon his death, the article continues: "'At last,' he uttered, in the penetrating accents of his authoritative voice, in the thick and guttural tones of his great days, which put aside all reply, these unforgettable words: 'I know that when I am dead, nothing of me will remain. I know I shall be nothing, Nothing, NOTHING.' He died twenty-four hours afterwards."

Is this all the consolation Haeckel has to offer his disciples? Is there any satisfaction in the knowledge of having all our strivings, toils, ambitions, affections, our All end in nothing?

In this connection the last words of other unbelievers might be of interest to our readers.

Voltaire, the noted French Infidel cried out upon his deathbed: "I must die, abandoned of God and man." To his infidel flatterers at his bedside he exclaimed: - "Leave me, I say — Begone — it is you who have brought me to my present condition. What a wretched glory you have produced in me." He hoped to allay his anguish by a written recantation; he had it prepared, signed, and saw it witnessed, but it was unavailing. His nurse exclaimed: "For all the wealth of Europe I would never see another infidel die."

A witness at the bedside of David Hume, the noted Deist, in commenting upon his disturbed sleeps, and more disturbed wakings, his involuntary breathings of remorse and frightful startings, stated that it was no difficult matter to determine that all was not right within. "I hope to God I shall never witness a similar scene," she exclaimed.

Thomas Paine, the author of the "The Age of Reason," a volume directed against atheism and against Christianity in favor of Deism cried out in despair: "My God, O my God, why hast Thou forsaken me," and these were his last recorded words.

Edward Gibbon, the noted historian and infidel, died in London in 1794. His last words were: "All is lost, finally irrevocably lost, all is dark and doubtful." He was expelled from Oxford for embracing Catholicism, remained a Catholic for eighteen months, later accepted Calvinism, but after a short period apostatized from both.

The Atheist Thomas Hobbes, whose system of psychology and morals were not only utterly antagonistic to Christianity, but to religion in general, died at Devonshire, England, in 1679. His last recorded words were: "I am about to take a leap in the dark."

Undoubtedly the last words of Haeckel will shortly be recorded, but in view of the foregoing, who would not rather exclaim with Balaam: "let me die the death of the Righteous, and let my last end be like his." Can anything be more awful than standing before the Judgment Bar of the great Jehovah whose very existence Haeckel denied?

What a contrast are the firm convictions of Job:

"I know that my Redeemer liveth, and that He shall stand at the latter day upon the earth, and though after my skin worms destroy this body, yet in my flesh shall I see God."

How glorious to be able to say "I know" in this vale of tears, even before the mists have been cleared away, and we see our Redeemer face to face!

The Truth-Seeker claims that it "neither affirms nor denies the immortality of the soul," but "waits for evidence."

From the title it has chosen for its paper it seems that the words of Timothy are very applicable: "ever learning, and never able to come to the knowledge of the truth." The fact that the truth is still being sought indicates clearly that it has not been found by *The Truth Seekers'* Editorial Staff as yet.

If the dividedness in the Christian denominations has something to do with the spread of Infidelity, and the acceptance of the theories of Haeckel, Darwin, Hume, Voltaire, and Gibbon, then why do not the atheists and agnostics agree among themselves? Do the Higher Critics agree? A volume entitled *The Higher Critics versus the Higher Critics* gives eloquent reply.

But why should all these theories trouble Christians, who stand upon the solid Rock of Holy Scripture, and with eyes of faith see "their title clear to mansions in the skies"? Has not the Lord's emphatic "Behold I have told you before" given them warning of these wolves in sheep's clothing who appear in the guise of learning?

May He in His infinite mercy give us grace and strength to stand steadfast in the faith once for all delivered to the saints, in these last perilous days when all the signs of the times indicate that the Judge is at the door, so that we may not be ashamed at His glorious appearing.

(Note: The last words of the infidels quoted are taken from a volume entitled "Dying Testimonies of Saved and Unsaved" by Rev. S. B. Shaw.)

ANNA HOPPE,
Milwaukee, Wis.[38]

Subsequent to these early years —after 1919— *The Northwestern Lutheran* carried no more editorials by Anna, publishing only her hymns and some related remarks. Her focus may have turned solely toward producing the undefined *Songs of the Church Year* contents. Perhaps her silence was advised or decided by the staff, with or without her awareness. Even if the incipient examples of her powerful lyricism lost their novelty, God saw that another audience would attune themselves to it: the Augustana Synod. This would come about through the benevolence of Adolf Hult.

Adolf Hult and the Augustana Connection

Adolf Hult came of age around Moline, Illinois, the son of Swedish pioneer Olof Hult, a blacksmith. After graduating from Augustana College in 1892, Adolf furthered his theological education at Augustana Theological Seminary. Upon receiving his Bachelor of Divinity, he was ordained in 1899, and called to his vicarage congregation, Messiah English Lutheran Church in Lake View, Illinois, part of the greater Chicago region. Eventually he did postgraduate work at the University of Chicago and taught Hebrew at nearby Chicago Lutheran Theological Seminary.[39] By 1908, the *Young Lutheran's Companion* appointed him associate editor. At Augustana College and Theological Seminary, he taught in the fields of Biblical theology, church history, symbolics, pastoral theology, and propedeutics (an introductory course into the discipline of theology).[40]

Hult personified the dynamic combination of both seminary training and choral music experience. For the season beginning in 1896, he directed the Svea Male Chorus in Moline, Illinois, an extension of the Swedish Lutheran Church Choir.[41] At Augustana College, Hult was listed as professor of church music and hymnology for the 1922-1923 school year.[42] The diamond-anniversary publication of First Lutheran Church in Moline—his home congregation—reported him as current president of the church choir and a member of the music committee and the men's society.[43] At the same time as the *Northwestern Lutheran* staff was sorting through a lode of Anna's hymnody, the *Lutheran Companion* was tending to Hult's unremitting idealism. During his term at the college and seminary, he wrote opinion pieces for the magazine on liturgical practice, choral music, education, and especially the concept of a unifying Lutheran hymnal.

Hult's unexpected friendship with Anna arose not at her initiative, but in a surprise envelope mailed to her from Illinois. Surely the faculty of Augustana Theological Seminary had kept up-to-date on current intersynodical events, and Hult along with his colleagues had read the inaugural *Northwestern Lutheran* issues. In 1934, Anna recalls this unforeseen advance:

About fifteen years ago, I penned "The Coming of the Nazarene", the theme being the Olivet discourse in which our Lord told of the destruction of the temple and His return to glory. This poem was published in *The Northwestern Lutheran* and later reproduced in *The Lutheran* of Philadelphia, which fell into the hands of Prof. Adolf Hult of Augustana Seminary, who at that time was a member of a committee compiling a new hymnal. Then came "the turn in the road."

With Hult being a professor at the Augustana Synod seminary, Anna might not have identified him right away as a hymnologist and future hymnal-committee member, whom she should befriend to spread her hymnic reach. Yet, he had noticed Anna's poetry published amongst the others—including other women—and contacted her. The *Lutheran Companion*'s initial reference to Anna is a 1917 reprint of her poem "To the Lutheran Church" from *The Northwestern Lutheran*.[44] Note of her acquaintance with Hult comes from his February 1919 description of the future Lutheran hymnbook, previously mentioned. Months after this essay, the editors printed her first poem, written for the opening of Augustana's Lutheran Bible Institute.

The Institute opened on February 3, 1919 at the site of First Lutheran Church in St. Paul. It was supervised by Dean Samuel Miller (pastor of Messiah Lutheran Church in Minneapolis) with part-time faculty members George N. Anderson, Roy F. Thelander, and Claus Wendell.[45] After Conrad Bergendorff declined to continue as professor in 1920, Carl J. Sodergren was asked to replace him and remained there for two decades directing the Institute's Expansion Department.[46] Through Sodergren's friendship with Hult, he became acquainted with Anna, and maintained correspondence with her. At this point, few English ministerial training schools existed, and the Augustana Synod—to which the Institute's pastors belonged—still conducted official business in Swedish. However, this new endeavor introduced itself as a program in the common American tongue for all Lutherans. It was endowed solely by donors and produced one hundred alumni by 1927.[47]

The Luth. Bible Institute,
St. Paul, Minn.

The Lutheran Bible Institute evening classes are now in full swing. About one hundred and fifty are enrolled in the two classes in St. Paul, and about fifty in the class in Minneapolis. We feel the great responsibility God has given us, and we plead with him to help us to keep all these interested in the things pertaining to Christ and His church.

The following poem was received on the day of opening of the Bible School from Anna Hoppe, a Lutheran friend in Milwaukee, Wis. It was read at the opening service.

DEDICATION
(To The Lutheran Bible Institute, St. Paul, Minn.)

Proceed! In Christ's dear Name, proceed!
Thou prayer-born Bearer of the Word of Truth!
Proceed! In Christ's dear name, proceed!
Illume the path of childhood, age, and youth!
Into the Light do thou the lightless guide.
Unfurl the banner of the Crucified!

Proceed! In Christ's dear name, proceed!
Fear not the scoffer's scorn, the skeptic's sneer!
But to the Master's blest command give heed,
And spread His glorious Gospel far and near!
Thou hast a Word to speak, O be not mute,
Thou precious, prayer-born Bible Institute!

Proceed! In Christ's dear Name, proceed!
The Father still can bless abundantly;
The tender Shepherd still His flock can feed;
The Holy Spirit still can pilot thee!
How blest the hope, how blest the promise sure,
God's Holy Word forever shall endure!

Proceed! In Christ's dear Name, proceed!
The glorious Truth of Saving Grace proclaim!
Sow thou in faith the precious Gospel seed,

And glorify the blest Redeemer's Name!
Defy the world's disdain, the critic's scorn,
Exalt the Son of God, the Virgin-born!

Proceed! In Christ's dear Name, proceed!
Continue in His strength the task begun!
With Bread Divine do thou the hungry feed,
Be thou content to know His will is done!
O what a glorious privilege is thine,
To flood earth's darkness with the Light Divine!

Proceed! In Christ's dear Name, proceed!
Thou prayer-born citadel of Truth, and may
The Triune God supply your every need,
Direct and guide you on the heaven-ward way!
O follow where the Risen Christ doth lead!
Proceed! In Christ's dear Name, Proceed! Proceed![48]

A year later, in the *Lutheran Companion*'s "Home Circle" section of December 4, 1920, Anna dedicated an Advent poem to Hult's wife, Edna.[49] Evidently they must have corresponded along with Anna's hymnological mailings, and Mrs. Hult took an interest in the young woman's work through her husband's report. Clearly the Hults kept up written correspondence with Anna, sharing hymns as well as other resources. Of her own inspiration, Anna reviewed Hult's Old Testament *Bible Primer,* a curriculum of Biblical narratives for younger Sunday School levels. This unsolicited accolade landed in an advertisement for the New Testament volume, which came out a year later. Anna is referred to as a "prominent writer of religious poetry and an active Sunday-school worker."

I found the Old Testament Primer a gem indeed worth its weight in gold and then some! The colorings are beautiful and the pictures very well chosen. It is one of the most beautiful volumes of its kind I have seen on the market in years, and I am sure the same can be said of the New Testament Primer which I have not had the pleasure to peruse as yet.

The author deserves the profoundest gratitude and heartiest congratulations of the Augustana Synod for his splendid work. He certainly understands the little folks and possesses the rare gift of conversing with them in a language and manner which gains their interest, attention, and confidence at the start, opens up the well-springs of childish imagination and leads these little lambs in the verdant pastures of God's Holy Word. The seed thus implanted will surely be blessed with fruitage by Him who said of these little ones, 'For of such is the Kingdom of Heaven.'

These remarks will probably seem somewhat out of place in an order sent to your commercial department, but having occasion to write you, I have taken the liberty to express my opinion of a literary treasure, the merit of which words fail to adequately express. It cannot be recommended too highly, and I am sure that all who possess the books, as well as prospective purchasers, will place their stamp of approval upon all I have stated. I certainly wish the Primers a wide circulation, for they richly deserve it."[50]

As the Augustana Synod commenced assembly of their 1925 hymnal, Hult addressed the desperate lack of "hymns for the Church Year of our church" in a 1921 article entitled "Our Primal Hymnal Need."[51] His visionary idea of an ultimate American-Lutheran hymnal did not settle with the hastened project of *Hymnal and Order of Service*. In a determined attempt, he may have written to Anna, proposing hymns on the lectionary as a new objective for her bimonthly verse. Hult probably recommended Anna's inclusion, pairing poems he found noteworthy with coordinating tunes. Aware of the number of her pieces, and realizing that the hymnal committee would be unable to accommodate the entire set, he may have proposed a further compendium, *Songs of the Church Year*, and forwarded the idea to the author herself. Consider how thrilled she must have been upon hearing that her very own book would be released! Over the years trailing its publication, they clearly continued to write, and he may be the unsung advocate for her hymnody.

His May 1943 obituary in *Concordia Theological Monthly* (an LCMS publication) commended his service as a confessional Lutheran.

With deep sorrow we read in *The Lutheran Companion* (Augustana Synod) that Dr. Adolf Hult, professor at the Augustana Seminary in Rock Island, Ill., has been taken from us. Ever since the day when we first read an article of his, we have belonged to the large circle of his admirers. He was a conservative Lutheran, standing firmly on the Scriptures and the Confessions, and his thoughts he expressed in forceful language reminding one of the diction of Carlyle. *The Lutheran Companion* states that the deceased "was not only a preacher and an editor but also a poet and a musician. His love for the highest and noblest form of church music and hymnody, particularly the Lutheran choral, as well as his staunch championship of Lutheran practices, contributed much in raising the standards of worship within the Augustana Synod and in wider circles." What always impressed us was his strong aversion to everything that savored of sham and cant [insincerity] and his unflinching championship of the old evangelical truth. If we are not altogether mistaken, it was he who made the statement that the grandest book which the Lutheran Church of America produced was Walther's *Law and Gospel*. May the memory of this gifted Lutheran leader help to keep alive in us the appreciation of the treasures we possess in our Lutheran literature and music. He died March 6, being a little more than 73 years old. He served as pastor of churches in Chicago and Omaha, and in 1916 he became professor of church history at Augustana Seminary, which position he held to the time of his death.[52]

Had Anna remained alive and well two years longer, she surely would have grieved the death of her friend, gathered a eulogy into rhyme, and presented it to his heirs. Probably to his surprise, she passed away in relative youth, at the age of fifty-two years to his seventy-one.

Surely he encountered her stellar words printed in *The Lutheran Companion* nearly a decade before. They will suffice as a memorial.

The untiring encouragement and ceaseless kindness of this musically gifted saint of God touched harp strings not hitherto attuned to hymnody, and there followed the *Songs of the Church Year*, and the hymns which followed the publication of this little book, and some ninety or so translations from the German. If Dr. Hult would step into a Quaker prayer-meeting, that group would arise and sing and ask for an organ! As a lover of Lutheran Church music and Lutheran hymns this lover of the Scriptures and Doctor of Divinity has no peer! Augustana Seminary students will say "Amen" to that. And he is peerless, too, in the encouragement of others. [53]

Mingling with Hult's contacts in the Augustana Synod brought Anna's hymns further than she had likely envisioned. Several of his former college and seminary classmates were published authors with Augustana Book Concern, editorial associates with *The Lutheran Companion* and the *Luther League Messenger*,[54] and leaders in both missionary efforts and local ministries of mercy.

Ernest E. Ryden

Another key friendship came about in Ernest Edwin Ryden. As a collaborator and personal friend of Hult, Ryden spent nearly his whole career furthering Lutheran journalism, driven with an ecumenical spirit which generated the formation of the Lutheran Church in America. Born in Kansas City, Missouri in 1886, his first experience in the field came as a police reporter there. Upon graduation of Augustana College and Seminary, he took his initial call to Holy Trinity Lutheran Church (Jamestown, New York) from 1914-1920, followed by Gloria Dei Lutheran Church in the affluent Highland Park neighborhood of St. Paul, Minnesota (1920-1934). Additionally, he led the new field of "camp pastor" or military chaplain for the Augustana Synod during World War I, stationed in in Spartanburg, South Carolina from 1917-1918.

Editing *The Lutheran Companion* from 1934-1961, Ryden continued his involvement begun in the 1920s as a contributor and associate.[55] During this time, the *Companion* hosted a weekly column acquainting its readers with a favorite hymn's story. Though no author is named, the expertise and conversational style sound similar to Ryden's. These lively studies became a radio program on KSTP (Minneapolis-St. Paul), aptly named "The Story of Our Hymns," which engaged Augustana members with their musical heritage. Though well received among Ryden's compatriots, his serial did not progress to national broadcast, but returned to print in a book of the same name (1930).[56]

As if this accomplishment was nothing at which to retire, Ryden's sundry posts included service on the Augustana College and synod Christian Education and Literature boards, committees for the *Hymnal and Order of Service* (1925), *Junior Hymnal* (1930) and *Service Book and Hymnal* (1958), time as president of the American Lutheran Conference (1938-1942), and an honorary Doctor of Divinity from his alma mater. As a result, his adaptable and brilliant personality would obtain decoration of the Royal Order of the North Star by the Swedish government in 1949.[57] He is distinguished in hymnology for unparalleled Scandinavian research, and in Lutheranism for his irenic approach to synodical boundaries. The convictions about liturgics and education which Hult had communicated in the press, Ryden brought to fruition in his diverse positions of influence.

When compiling *The Story of Our Hymns*, historical sketches encompassing all of Christian hymnody, Ryden highlighted stories from leaders in his generation. Anna, a close friend to his hymn-appreciating company, fit the model nicely. Since he collected the following biography from her own written interview responses, his accounts and her 1934 memoirs may be our only firsthand information about her available today.

As like-minded colleagues, he and Anna appear to have been fond of each other. They were born but two years apart, and shared the pursuits of hymnwriting, translation, and evangelism. Many letters of their faithful encouragements passed between St. Paul and Milwaukee, and one is left to wonder what more he learned of Anna's story through them.

A Lutheran Psalmist of Today

It is gratifying to know that the spirit of hymnody is not dead, and that still today consecrated men and women are being inspired to "sing new songs unto Jehovah." In Milwaukee, Wis., lives a young woman who for several years has been attracting wide-spread attention by her Christian lyrics. Her name is Anna Hoppe, and the hymns she writes suggest strongly something of the style and spirit of the Lutheran hymns of a by-gone age.

Born of German parents in Milwaukee in 1889, she began to write verse in early childhood. Most of them were on patriotic themes, such as Washington, Lincoln, The Battle of Gettysburg, and Paul Jones. "At the age of about eleven," Miss Hoppe tells us, "I wrote a few lines on Angels."

It was at the age of twenty-five years, however, that she began in earnest the writing of spiritual poetry. Many of her poems were published in religious periodicals and aroused much interest. In the hymnal of the Augustana Synod, published in 1925, twenty-three of her hymns were included. Since that time a collection of her hymns under the title, *Songs of the Church Year*, has appeared. In 1930 eight of her lyrics were published in the *American Lutheran Hymnal*.

As a prolific writer of hymns, Miss Hoppe probably has no equal in the Lutheran Church today. Her unusual talent seems all the more remarkable when it is known that she is practically self-educated. After she had finished the eighth grade in the Milwaukee public schools, she entered a business office. Since that time she has worked continuously, and has received the benefit of only a few months' training at evening schools. At present she is employed in the office of the Westinghouse Company.

Her hymns are composed in the midst of the stress and hurry of modern life. "Many of my hymns," she writes, "have been written on my way to and from church, and to and from work. I utilize my lunch hours for typing the hymns and keeping up correspondence. I used to do quite a bit of writing on Sunday afternoons, but now we have a Layman's Hour in our church at that time, and I do not like to miss it. I also attend our Fundamentalist Bible lectures, Jewish mission meetings, and the like. Still I find a minute here and there in which to jot down some verse."

Although few of Miss Hoppe's hymns rise to heights of poetic rapture, they are characterized by a warmth of feeling and fervency of spirit that make them true lyrics. They are thoroughly Scriptural in language, although they sometimes become too dogmatic in phraseology. A deep certainty of faith, however, breathes through their lines and saves them from becoming prosaic.

One of her most beautiful hymns is for New Year's. Its opening stanza reads:

Jesus, O precious Name,
By heaven's herald spoken,
Jesus, O holy Name,
Of love divine the token.
Jesus, in Thy dear Name
This new year we begin;
Bless Thou its opening door,
Inscribe Thy Name within.

A hymn for Epiphany reflects something of the same spirit of adoration:

Desire of every nation,
Light of the Gentiles, Thou!
In fervent adoration
Before Thy throne we bow;
Our hearts and tongues adore Thee,
Blest Dayspring from the skies.
Like incense sweet before Thee,
Permit our songs to rise.

The final stanza of her Ascension hymn is full of poetic fire:

Ascend, dear Lord!
Thou Lamb for sinners slain,
Thou blest High Priest, ascend!
O King of kings, in righteousness e'er reign,
Thy kingdom hath no end.

Thy ransomed host on earth rejoices,
While angels lift in song their voices.
Ascend, dear Lord!

Her fidelity to Scriptural language may be seen in the following simple verses:

Have ye heard the invitation,
Sinners ruined by the fall?
Famished souls who seek salvation,
Have ye heard the loving call?
Hark! a herald of the Father
Bids you of His supper taste.
Round the sacred table gather;
All is ready; sinners, haste!

O ye chosen, have ye slighted
This sweet call to you proclaimed?
Lo! the King hath now invited
All the halt, the blind, the maimed:
Come, ye poor from out the highways,
Come, a feast awaits you, come!
Leave the hedges and the byways,
Hasten to the Father's home.

We have heard Thee call, dear Father,
In Thy Word and sacrament;
Round Thy festal board we'll gather
Till our life's last day is spent.
Ours the risen Saviour's merit,
Ours the bounties of Thy love,
Ours Thy peace, till we inherit
Endless life in heaven above.

Miss Hoppe speaks in glowing terms of the spiritual impressions received in childhood from pious parents and a consecrated pastor, the sainted John Bading, who both baptized and confirmed her. Her father died in 1910.

"He was a very pious Lutheran," she writes, "and so is mother. They often spoke of afternoon prayer meetings they attended in Germany."

Some of her hymns not already mentioned are, "By nature deaf to things divine," "Heavenly Sower, Thou hast scattered," "How blest are they who through the power," "Lord Jesus Christ, the children's Friend," "O dear Redeemer, crucified," "O precious Saviour, heal and bless," "O'er Jerusalem Thou weepest," "Precious Child, so sweetly sleeping," "Repent, the Kingdom draweth nigh," "The Sower goeth forth to sow," "Thou camest down from heaven on high," "Thou hast indeed made manifest," "Thou Lord of life and death," "Thou virgin-born incarnate Word," "O Lord, my God, Thy holy law," "Jesus, Thine unbounded love," "He did not die in vain," "I open wide the portals of my heart," "Rise, my soul, to watch and pray," "O joyful message, sent from heaven," "O Thou who once in Galilee," and "Thou goest to Jerusalem." She is the translator of "O precious thought! some day the mist shall vanish," a hymn from the Swedish, as well as some eighty gems from German hymnody. Thirty-two of her German translations appeared in *The Selah Song Book,* edited by Adolf T. Hanser in 1922.

Many of Miss Hoppe's hymns have been written on the pericopes of the Church Year. She has consistently refused to have her hymns copyrighted, believing that no hindrance should be put in the way of any one who desires to use them.

Up to 1930 nearly 400 hymns had appeared from Miss Hoppe's pen. Her ambition is to write a thousand original Christian lyrics. [58]

The 1959 revision of Ryden's book, appearing after Anna's lifetime, bore the title *The Story of Christian Hymnody* and contained the following updates:

One of the most prolific of 20th century American women hymnwriters was Miss Anna Bernardine Hoppe of Milwaukee, Wis., who during the 1920s and 1930s contributed a large number of hymns to various hymnals. The daughter of German immigrants, she began to compose verse at the age of eleven, when she wrote a poem on angels. Although she had no more than an eighth grade education and found it necessary to support herself by working in a business office, she continued to cultivate her gift as a writer, and soon began to attract attention by her poetry.

"Many of my hymns, she once wrote, "have been written on my way to and from church, and to and from work. I utilize my lunch hours for typing the hymns and keeping up correspondence. I used to do quite a bit of writing on Sunday afternoons, but now we have a Laymen's Hour in our church at that time, and I do not like to miss it... Still I find a minute here and there in which to jot down some verse."

In 1925, no less than twenty-three of Miss Hoppe's hymns were published in *The Hymnal* of the Augustana Lutheran Church, and in 1930 eight were included in the *American Lutheran Hymnal*. In 1927, a collection of her hymns was published under the title, Hymns of the Church Year. One of her Lenten hymns, "O'er Jerusalem Thou weepest," has this moving stanza:

> O Thou Lord of my salvation,
> Grant my soul Thy blood-bought peace.
> By Thy tears of lamentation
> Bid my faith and love increase.
> Grant me grace to love Thy Word,
> Grace to keep the message heard,
> Grace to own Thee as my Treasure,
> Grace to love Thee without measure.

Other hymns by Miss Hoppe are "The Sower goeth forth to sow," "Rise arise! Rise arise!" "Jesus, O precious Name," "Precious Child, so sweetly sleeping," "Thou Lord of life and death," "O Father mine, whose mercies never cease," and "How blest are they who through the power." An Epiphany hymn, "Desire of every nation," is exceptionally fine.

Miss Hoppe also translated a large number of German hymns into English, and at least one Norwegian—Wexel's "O precious thought, some day the mist shall vanish."[59] It was her expressed ambition to write a thousand original Christian lyrics, and she probably composed at least one-half that number. She died in 1941.[60]

Hearing the St. Olaf Choir

At some point, Anna must have attended a concert by the St. Olaf Choir, perhaps May 8, 1920 at Augustana's auditorium during their extensive eastern choir tour.[61] For the first time, Lutheran chorales were particularly highlighted, circulating hymns with which Anna would have been familiar throughout the concert halls of America. Hult also attended the concert, stirred at the idea of a potential renaissance of Lutheran arts.[62] Perhaps Anna was his guest.

The program was as follows:

Blessing, Glory and Wisdom—Georg Gottfried Wagner[63]
Praise to the Lord—Sohren, arr. F. Melius Christiansen
Built on the Rock—Lindeman, arr. F.M.C.
A Mighty Fortress—Luther, arr. F. Melius Christiansen

The Word of God—Grieg
Savior of Sinners—Mendelssohn
O God, Hear My Prayer—Gretchaninoff

Father, Most Holy—Crueger
Hosanna—F.M.C.
Beautiful Savior—Folk melody, arr. F.M.C.
Wake, Awake—Nicolai, arr. F.M.C. [64]

Anna's poem reminisces:

The Northfield Choristers

I hear them still—the sweet, melodious singers,
The Luth'ran choristers—St. Olaf Choir!
Still in my heart the lovely music lingers,
Indeed a Seraph must have tuned the lyre!
As wafted to the earth on angels' pinions,
My soul doth hear the choral strains again,

It seems the choirs in yonder blest dominions
Breathed o'er the earth a grand, sublime Amen!

I hear them still—the harbingers of gladness!
Has David's harp come down from realms afar?
Or has the Psalmist come to hush earth's sadness,
And, in descending, left the gates ajar?
Sweet strains of melody, as if from Heaven,
Brood o'er the harp-strings of my troubled heart;
What sweet enchantment hath their music given!
What peace divine, of Heaven's calm a part!

Sing on! Thrill mankind with the Gospel story!
Tell troubled souls, "The Just shall live by Faith!"
Let weary pilgrims hear of rest and glory,
In spheres on high, beyond the gates of death!
Lead sinners to the Cross on Calv'ry's mountain;
To famished hearts the Bread of Life bestow!
Tell thirsty mortals of the crystal Fountain,
Where streams of living water ever flow![65]

The Musical Leader, a weekly Chicago-based periodical running
from 1900-67, published the same poem, accompanied by the note:

Dedicated to the St. Olaf Choir

Leading Lutherans and musicians have just received copies of a poem dedicated to the members of the famous
St. Olaf Choir of Northfield, Minn., which they regard as
an eloquent expression of the choir's inspirational power.

The poem, by Anna Hoppe of Milwaukee, tells most
clearly the remarkable influence that has come to St. Olaf
Choir, particularly during the period of its development
under the direction of Prof. F. Melius Christiansen. [66]

Adolf Hanser

Adolf T. Hanser—an Augustana pastor in Buffalo, New York—
published many Sunday school curricula, catechisms, and Bible
storybooks independently through Sotarion Publishing Company.

His venture of arranging an English and German hymnal together with notation was wholly self-edited.

Hult may have recommended Anna to his co-worker in the ministry and hymnody for her smart eye toward translation, and they shared a substantial part of the duties. At some point, Anna expressed her dissatisfaction regarding her own skills to Hanser. She received this letter of encouragement:

Buffalo, N.Y. Nov. 6 1920.

Miss. Anna Hoppe,
Milwaukee, Wisc.

Dear Co-worker,
Your judgement of your ability in regard of translating hymns is certainly not just to yourself. However, that is generally an asset, when we underestimate our own gifts. You certainly have a very large capacity for translating as shown in the work you now have sent me. Only to-day I received a letter from a pastor, who says that some translations in our hymnals are "hardly more than combination of lines ending in riming words." That is putting it very strong. But it shows that our pastors are taking more notice of these matters than formerly. This man is very much interested in our new book and urges us like many other letters we receive every week to hurry the completion of the book. That man will be delighted with your translation. I am also mentioning this in order to show you that the work I am doing and in which I am delighted to say now have your valuable cooperation, is not simply a personal hobby, but that we are meeting a demand which is at the present time greater than ever.

There let me urge you to kindly drop the idea, that you cannot translate, but give this work, for which the harvest is also white but has very, very few good laborers your best attention.

I must congratulate you on the stirring poem in the "American Lutheran." It gave me great pleasure that these people [gave] you the front page, so no one would miss it. They are wide awake these publicity people and know a good thing, when they see it.

Regarding your apology of not confining yourself to a literal translation, but using freedom in rendering certain verses, I assure you that this is the proper thing to do. The point is to get a good verse which can be sung easily. The best translators use this freedom. Often a verse is actually improved thereby. So, do not bind yourself at all to every detail of the original, but follow your own judgement. For the same reason it is not necessary to translate every verse. In some otherwise good hymns the verses are very inferior. Again, they have nothing to do with the theme. In fact, often the logic is broken by a verse which may have a fine thought and excellent poetry but is not in harmony with the original thought.

Now I will be looking to you for further translation. If there is a special hymn, which you think ought to be translated please let me hear from you in regard to it. I may have a translation. Otherwise it will be only proper for you to undertake the work of translation. For there is an advantage to work on something you have chosen yourself. And in thanking you for your valuable help I am

Most gratefully yours,
Adolf Hanser.[67]

In its issue of December 10, 1922, *The Northwestern Lutheran* reviewed Hanser's collection, containing 450 hymns in all. Editor John Jenny recognized Anna's assistance, "There are over 30 hymns... appearing in English translation for the first time, in this collection, among these 29 hymns translated by Miss Anna Hoppe, the latter of which have graced the columns of *The Northwestern Lutheran...*"[68]

The redistribution of Anna's reliable verse seems to have been of a lavish amount. Designed mindfully for the younger set of Augustana, *My Church: An Illustrated Lutheran Manual* came out annually, sketching scenes of synodical ventures. Vivid accounts and photographs showing missions abound, so this inclusion by their Wisconsin Synod collaborator is not out of place. As noted above, an earlier version of this hymn in *The American Lutheran* initially drew Hult's attention.

The Coming of the Nazarene
By Anna Hoppe.

Music fills the Kidron valley, a song has just begun,
"Hosanna in the highest! Hosanna, David's Son!"
The shouts are coming nearer, see the procession now,
Behold the palm-tree branches on Olivet's fair brow!
For whom this great commotion? For whom this jubilee?
"Jesus is here, the prophet! Jesus of Galilee?
"Hosanna in the highest, O wondrous, joyous scene!"
Art thou so highly honored, Thou lowly Nazarene?"

Lo, they have reached the hilltop, and now His eyes behold
The Holy City's beauty, the temple with its gold;
He sees the palm-tree branches, He hears the shouts, the cheers,
But Thou, beloved city, hast filled His eyes with tears!
"Hosanna in the highest," the song of triumph swells,
But of the solemn story the Master's sorrow tells!
He speaks, the olive branches bow to the mournful tone,
"If Thou hadst known, fair city, if only thou hadst known."

The toil of day is over, Judea's sun has set,
Its parting rays illumine the heights of Olivet,
Its glory fills the valley, its crimson afterglow
Is mirrored in the waters of Kidron's stream below.
Slowly, with His chosen few, the Nazarene appears,
His eyes divine, so mournful, so often filled with tears,
See in prophetic vision the Temple rent in twain,
Its mighty pillars fallen — its crumbling ruins remain.

The lips divine have uttered a solemn prophecy,
And eager hearts inquire, "Master, when shall it be?"
He speaks, a solemn stillness falls o'er Mount Olivet,
"Ye shall hear of wars, beloved, but the end is not yet,
For nation against nation shall rise, and ye shall hear
Of famines, pestilences, and earthquakes far and near,
But that great day and hour, when from My Father's throne
I come to judge the nations, to mortals is not known."

The twilight shadows linger about the distant west,
The chosen few are weary, the Master longs for rest;
But oh, Thy words, dear Savior, shall through the ages ring
Until Thy ransomed thousands behold Thee as their King.
Until they see Thy glory, Thou Lamb on Calvary slain,
Once Thou didst come to suffer, Oh, come again to reign!
When in Thy pow'r and glory we see Thee in the sky,
No more shall glad Hosannas be changed to "Crucify."

I see Thy words, dear Saviour, Thy prophecies fulfilled,
As o'er earth's warring nations Thy Father's wrath is spilled,
Signs of Thy great appearing shine forth in ages past,
And all creation groaneth, "Wilt Thou not come at last?"
Master, Thy saints are sighing, "When will the night be o'er?"
When wilt Thou send Thy message, "There shall be time
    no more?"
When wilt Thou still the longing of my impatient heart
To see Thee in Thy beauty, to see Thee as Thou art?"[69]

From time to time, Anna's verses sprung up in *The Lutheran Companion,* either by Hult's reference or her own submission. While she must have composed the following wedding hymn for a summer 1922 celebration, it could be that Augustana friends were present and recommended its inclusion, or that *The Northwestern Lutheran* had no interest in its specialized character. Arranged to fit the meter of Richard Wagner's famous chorus, this example offered a worthy alternative for the church ceremony and might have been sung as the processional.

A Pastoral Wedding Hymn.

By Anna Hoppe.

Tune: "Bridal Chorus" from *Lohengrin* by R. Wagner.

O praise the Lord this hallowed day,
As to His altar ye wend your glad way.
With grateful hearts His goodness bless,
His loving kindness and mercy confess.

He Who from mother's arms to this hour.
Kept you by His omnipotent power,
Still can support you, protect you, guide you.
With all your needs His love can provide you;
In Christ, the Father calls you His own!
Come with rejoicing before His throne!

O praise the Lord this hallowed day.
As to His altar ye wend your glad way.
With grateful hearts His goodness bless.
His loving kindness and mercy confess,
His mercy confess.

As holy bonds unite you,
That naught but death shall part,
May heav'nly peace delight you.
Abiding in each heart!

In Jesus Name your task begin,
He Who redeemed you, your labors shall bless.
The Comforter, Who dwells within,
Shall grant you solace when trials oppress.

Serving the Saviour from day to day.
His holy favor bless all your way!
May ye find joy and holy elation,
Spreading the tidings of free salvation.
Telling the lost ones Jesus can save!
God give you courage! God make you brave!
God bless you both! God bless your troth!

God bless your footsteps wherever you roam,
His Holy Word with you abide,
Till Jesus calls you to His heav'nly Home,
Heaven's Home Sweet Home.

Milwaukee. [70]

In 1927, the Augustana Synod produced the seventh volume of its *Missionary Calendar*, a book educating members regarding their synod's home missions, foreign missions, and individual missionaries. Along with student editor Ewald B. Lawson and Joseph Lonnquist, both seminary seniors, Adolf Hult and his distant protégé Anna contributed poetry concerning this topic.[71] The more notable of her works attained places in other Augustana hymnals, such as the *Junior Hymnal* (1928) and *Concordia Hymnal* (1933), and various shorter Sunday School song treasuries.

In addition, Anna remained in tune with the affairs of her sister synod, Missouri. In the *Milwaukee Journal* issue of June 6, 1931, evidence of her association with another Missouri Synod congregation surfaces in a commemoratory poem.

Cross Lutheran Congregation Forsakes Old Edifice for New
Verses Written to Old Edifice
First Services to Be Held in Modern Structure Sunday

Farewell, dear old temple, we leave thee forever!
No more will our songs in thy precincts arise.
But can we forget thee? Ah never, no never!
Too sweet are the mem'ries, too tender the ties!

There will be tugs at many heartstrings Sunday when members of Cross Lutheran church, one of Milwaukee's pioneer congregations, forsake the fine old edifice at Sixteenth st. and Fond du Lac av., where they have worshipped for more than 50 years, to enter and dedicate a new and modern church at Sixteenth and Vine sts. Miss Anna Hoppe, Milwaukee Lutheran hymnologist, has caught some of the sentiment of the occasion in a farewell poem, the first stanza of which appears above. The old church of which she sings has been a west side landmark for years. One of its chief features is a lofty steeple, with a clock on each of its four sides, visible for many blocks.

Farewell Service Held

The spire has not been overlooked in the farewell verses. Miss Hoppe refers to it in another stanza:

"The cross on thy spire, pointing skyward to heaven,
So silently preached of the homeland on high,
Where rest everlasting to wand'rers is given,
Where pleasure eternal bid sorrows goodby."

Church members, however, have already said goodby to the old church. They held a farewell service there last Sunday. Tomorrow, for the first time, services will be held in the new edifice, with Rev. E. F. Schueler, pastor, officiating.

The first service, at 9 a.m., will be addressed by Dr. Frederick Brand, St. Louis, who will speak in German, and the Rev. Louis J. Sieck, also of St. Louis, who will give an English sermon. The Rev. Martin Strasen, Shawano, and the Rev. O.F. Engelbrecht, Milwaukee, will preach at an afternoon service at 3 o'clock and the Rev. O.A. Geisemann, River Forest, Ill., will be heard at an evening worship service at 7:30 p.m.[72]

For the 1930 meeting of the Delegate Synod of the Wisconsin and Missouri Synods, Anna greeted the members of her synodical fellowship with a benedictory hymn. The text, as follows, was published in *The Lutheran Witness*.

To Our Guests, the Delegate Synod.

Hail, brethren! We extend a hearty greeting
And bid you welcome with a hand-clasp true!
God bless you! May He bless our hallowed meeting,
And may His glorious grace abound toward you!
Coworkers in the vineyard of the Saviour,
Ye who have borne the heat of toilsome days,
Come ye apart awhile, bask in His favor,
Rest in His love and sing Him songs of praise.

Miles may divide, but Christian faith unites us
In sweet communion at the throne of grace,
Where every day the Father's love delights us
And wings of fervent prayer span all the space.
But now in Jesus' name we warmly greet you,
Who for His sake have come from near and far.
How blest the privilege to know and meet you!
How sweet the joy to see you as you are!

You have gone forth in heaven-born devotion
The everlasting Gospel to proclaim
In homeland field, in lands across the ocean—
Salvation full and free in Jesus' name.
God bless the seed you sowed beside all waters,
Throughout the vastness of His harvest-field!
In fruitful hearts of Zion's sons and daughters
May it spring up and boundless fruitage yield!

The days are dark, but in the darkness shining
Is God's eternal light, His saving Word.
In His dear hands the Church's cause resigning,
In changing times we have a changeless Lord.
O may we all, illumined by His Spirit,
For our appointed tasks new courage take,
Trust in His Word, revere it, preach it, hear it!
His Word abides though all things earthly shake.

God speed you, brethren, on your homeward journey,
When, sessions ended, we must say, "Good-by!"
God bless and keep you through time's troubled tourney
Until we meet in yonder realm on high![73]

Carl J. Sodergren (1870-1949), a colleague of Hult, had been a professor at Augustana Theological Seminary, editorial associate of *The Lutheran Companion*, and director of the Lutheran Bible Institute. Evidently, Sodergren and Anna became aware of one another through the Adolf Hult connection during this time, meeting perhaps after the publication of her book. Anna eagerly mailed him a letter, discussing hymnody, feeling inferior as a poet, and recent exciting events. The next day, he typed this effervescent update:

The Lutheran Bible Institute
1619 Portland Avenue
Minneapolis, Minnesota
Samuel Miller, Dean

Feb. 15, 1931

Miss Anna Hoppe
2122-C No. 16th St.,
Milwaukee, Wis.

My dear Miss Hoppe!

Your Epistle to the Sodergrens was received and read
with interested delight upon my arrival yesterday, and because it contained no secrets of State, I took the liberty
of passing it on to my old sweetheart who finished her
reading by singing out, "My, but she must be a wonderful
Woman!" And for once I didn't contradict her!!

There were not "too many stanzas" in your prose poem this
time. Your "inspiration" was "sustained thruout." But if you
think I'm going to write 6 pp. by way of a reply, you're very
much mistaken. I'm so tired this evening—after preaching
in Excelsior, Minn., again today—that I'm going to dismiss
you curtly with a mere acknowledgment. But I wish you
knew how grateful that acknowledgment is.

Nor am I going to try to tell you how happy I am to have
been enabled to realize my cherished hope of years and
years to meet you face to face. It was a Red Letter Day in
my young life. I'm afraid that my ugly headache spoiled
your good (?) impressions. I sure was a sick affair by the
time I had to say goodbye. And I realize what a sorry
figure I must have appeared to you. But I know you are
"considering the source" and will make allowances for
human frailty.

My Bible Conference proved to be the Lord's Conference.
He "took charge" and rained "showers of blessing" upon
us. The church was jammed to the doors every evening,

and the "response" was <u>inspiring.</u> How grateful I am for the grace that sustained me thruout to minister to these souls with "the Word of Truth." Thank you, dear friend, for your faithful intercession!

Had lunch downtown with our mutual "Adolph" yesterday. He was here addressing the (Norwegian) Luther Seminary, but left so promptly that he didn't have time to come out to our home. One favorite topic of conversation during the speeding minutes was a mutually very dear friend in Milwaukee. But you'll have to guess the rest.

"Miss Havergal"? Yes, you're <u>related</u> all right. But she's only your second cousin. In other words, your Muse is far superior to hers. Possibly not <u>all</u> that you have written, but about 20 of your best leaves her far behind. Especially some of your <u>latest</u> ones. Because you are growing by leaps and bounds. And just because God have given you the "gift supernal" I wish that you would wait for your moments of <u>inspiration,</u> and then take time to chisel those fewer productions into immortal classics. You are too prolific for the <u>quality</u> of which you are capable. Some day when I get shelved and have time to breathe I'm going to pick out the diamonds and pearls from among the semi-precious stones and suggest their publication. They are going to <u>live.</u>

We are so happy to know that you could attend that harp concert and for what it must have meant to you. And even tho you were disappointed in that one respect, I know that even that classical secular music glorified the divine Source, of all beauty, in every devout heart.

Congratulations on that windfall of Miss Havergal's works! I trust you will be permitted to cancel the other order.

Must close now—tho I sure don't <u>want</u> to. Mrs. Sodergren wishes to be remembered to you. She was cheered by your kind words. So was her hubby.

Thanking you for—O for everything—for those deeply precious invisible gifts which never can be expressed in mere words.

Sincerely Your "elder brother" in Christ,
C. J. Sodergren[74]

Carl Doving became another noteworthy colleague and correspondent of Anna's through their Scandinavian-Lutheran network. After *Songs of the Church Year* came out, he was among the favored to receive a signed copy.[75] She respected his work as a linguist, translator, and hymnologist, offering the following praise in *The American Lutheran.*

Dr. Martin Luther's Spiritual Songs
By Anna Hoppe

Volumes have been written on what the Reformation has meant to civil and religious liberty, and what the Bible has meant to the world. A very interesting and inspiring exhibit at the Hall of Religion in Chicago's Century of Progress reveals the fact that his Small Catechism has reached the phenomenal record of translation into 145 languages! One hundred and twenty-three actual copies are in possession of Dr. Tanner of the Norwegian Lutheran Church of America. The stupendous task of gathering these specimens was accomplished by Dr. Carl Doving, venerable institutional missionary of Chicago, who for years carried on an extensive correspondence with every nook and corner of the globe in hymnal research work. The world-famous Doving Library of Hymnody embraces more than 300 languages and dialects!

In connection with the Luther Anniversary Jubilee it is surely timely to make mention of the great Reformer as a hymnwriter and his influence on Protestant hymnody. The hymns which gushes forth from his heart literally sang the Gospel into the hearts of the peasantry, and widely influenced the spread of the glad tiding of a full and free salvation—justification by faith. His foes admitted that his songs did more than his preaching in the accomplishment of this end. Our readers will surely be amazed at the result of Dr. Carl Doving's world-wide hymnological survey, covering hymns of the great Reformer, extending over a period of years, an authentic review of which follows:

"Ein Feste Burg ist unser Gott"—("A Mighty Fortress Is Our God") the battle-hymn of the Reformation—has been translated into 175 languages and dialects! No other hymn written after the birth of Christ has been translated into so many languages. Dr. Doving is authority for saying that this hymn has been translated into 42 European languages, 51 tongues spoken in Asia, 60 of those used in Africa, 9 American languages, one of the Australian Bush, and 12 of those spoken in Oceania.

"Ein feste Burg" in one hundred seventy-five languages and dialects, every continent on earth represented, every race telling of the victory of God's Eternal Word over every foe of humanity—what a stupendous thought! Eternity alone will reveal how many have been brought to faith in Christ by means of the old, old story told in song.

Dr. Martin Luther did not consider himself a hymn-writer, still four hundred years after his first hymn was composed, Dr. Doving discovered that four of his hymns had been translated into more than fifty languages.

The beautiful Christmas hymn, "Good News From Heaven The Angels Bring," has been translated into 72 languages; "Out of the Depths I Cry To Thee," into 67; "All Praise To Thee Eternal Lord," into 55; "Come, Holy Spirit, God and Lord," into 47; "Lord Keep Us Steadfast In Thy Word," into 31; "Christ Jesus Lay In Death's Strong Bands," in 25. His metrical version of the Nicene Creed has been translated 33 times and the versification of the Lord's Prayer, 32 times. His hymn "These Are The Blessed Ten Commands," has had 26 translations.

Christendom's harp hung mutely on the willows during the Dark Ages. Luther brought it down and its celestial strings have since flooded the earth with melodies rising heavenward like sweet incense, from every kindred and tongue and people and nation—for wherever the Everlasting Gospel brings the certainty of pardon, peace, and joy, and the assurance of life eternal to the sinner, there will be "psalms and hymns and spiritual songs,"

All the great writers of evangelical hymnody since the glorious Reformation have been influenced by Luther's psalmody, and neither Modernism nor the powers of hell will be able to silence the rhapsodies of a singing faith. May He "Who giveth songs in the night" give us all a true appreciation of the treasure we as the "Singing Church" possess in our solacing, faith-strengthening, joy-bringing, triumphant hymns![76]

Personal and Occasional Works

Letters like Sodergren's were highlights of Anna's daily activities. To be sure, she interacted with co-workers at the office, greeted friends in the fellowship of church, and conversed with her parents and siblings at home. Yet, imagine returning from a day of typing, filing, and answering calls to find a note from a leading hymnal editor in a distant state! Correspondence via the postal service constituted her most important communication—it was the means by which her hymns traveled, and thereby introduced her to new associates in superior places.

While her literary talent may have most brightly shone forth from hymnals, papers, and periodicals, it also found its place in general Christian life, serving the daily activities and special occasions in lives of friends. Ample mentions are made of her contacts and encouragements outside by letter and face-to-face, though their direct documentation is scarcely recorded.

The Northwestern Lutheran and *The Lutheran Companion* most predominantly displayed Anna's new hymns throughout the 1920s. However, *The American Lutheran* remained cognizant of her busy pen, and two new offerings appeared on the way to *Songs of the Church Year*. In addition to her 1924 jubilee hymn commemorating the first Lutheran hymnal's 400th anniversary, this translation appeared in a celebratory issue of *The American Lutheran*.

Praise the Lord

Praise the Lord in Temples holy;
Night is past—the light unfurled!
God spake to the Savior lowly:
"Shine, Thou Light of all the World!"

Praise the Lord! From dark abysses
Darkness rose to veil the day,
But His Word the winds addresses
And the storm-clouds flee away!

Praise the Lord! The Light still beameth,
Christ, the Sun, in radiant glow!
O'er the earth His brightness gleameth
Joy and blessing to bestow!

Raise the stain, and swell the chorus!
Sing "A Fortress is our God!"
Luther sings the anthem glorious
With the choirs in Heav'n's abode!

CARL GLAESER
Translated by ANNA HOPPE.[77]

Another festive Pentecost season poem greeted readers on the cover
of the June 1926 issue.

"Go-Tell!"

"Go, tell His disciples and Peter
He is risen from the dead"
To the women at the tomb-door
The heavenly herald said.
And they sped away in rapture—
They who loved their Lord so well,
And the angel's word re-echoed:
"Fear not. He is risen. Go—tell!"

The tidings so willingly carried
Soon spread o'er mountain and plain;
The hills and dales of Judea
Rang out with the glorious strain.
All Galilee with rejoicing

Sang praise to Immanuel,
As the news came o'er the waters:
"Fear not. He is risen. Go—tell!"

O wonderful, wonderful message,
What comfort thou dost impart!
What cheer to the troubled spirit!
What balm to the wounded heart!
Still today the music wafted
From the ringing Sabbath bell
Tells the story of salvation:
"Fear not. He is risen. Go—tell!"

Once He died on Calvary's mountain—
Christ Jesus, the Son of God,
And purchased the world's redemption
With His holy, precious Blood.
Over sin and death victorious
He conquered the powers of hell.
Now His Word proclaims our freedom—
"Fear not. I am risen. Go—tell!"

"Go tell it to tots in the cradle!
Let school-children hear the truth!
Tell it from pulpit and altar,
And inspire the hearts of youth!
Go, tell it unto thy manhood—
To the rich and the poor as well!
Tell it to the old and feeble!
Go, tell it! Go, tell it! Go—tell!"

Forgiveness, and peace, and sweet solace
The soul-stirring message brings,
As it now descends from Heaven
Where He reigns as King of Kings!
And they who in faith receive it
Forever with Him shall dwell.
O Church of Christ, He entreats Thee—
"Fear not. I am risen. Go—tell!"

Fear not! He is with thee forever,
For thou art His chosen bride!
He is risen! Death is vanquished!
The tomb-door is open wide!
Go, tell the nations the story;
Break down Satan's citadel!
Till the harvest-fields are garnered
Go, tell it! Go, tell it! Go—tell!

O lift up the Cross of he Savior,
And keep His Banner unfurled
Till His wonderful Evangel
Has reached all the wide, wide world!
Till His wheat is in the store-house,
And He tells thee all is well,
Let thy word and pen proclaim;
Go, tell it! Go, tell it! Go—tell!

Anna Hoppe, Milwaukee, Wis.[78]

In her personal collection at the Milwaukee Historical Society, dated January 25, 1921, Anna extends "A Call to the Children of Luther." Uniquely, her hymnody often commemorates Lutheran history as its effects are felt in the 20th century, and Luther's life is a common theme—integrating her earlier patriotic themes with the church year.

Arise, ye heirs of Gospel truth and freedom!
Lift high the banner of your Lord and King!
And to the Hero, coming forth from Edom,
Anthems of praise, and royal tribute bring!
Arise, and crown the Conqueror victorious!
The King of Kings, the mighty Lord of Lords!
For lo, He comes with laurels, priceless, glorious!
Eternal liberty His reign affords!

O fear no more Jehovah's condemnation!
And tremble not when Horeb's thunders roar!
Behold, the Crucified has brought salvation!
On Calv'ry's Cross the Law's dread curse He bore!

Forgiveness, mercy, grace, and Life immortal,
His love bestows. His precious blood sufficed
To open wide the glorious heav'nly portal!
O hail with joy your blest Redeemer, Christ!

Arise, ye children of the heav'nly Father!
Tell all the world of His so boundless love!
Fear not beneath the Cross of Christ to gather,
With heart and lips your fervent troth to prove!
Led by His Spirit, boldly make confession,
And hail the Son of God the Lord of All!
Deny all earthly foes and hell's oppression!
Boldly sound forth the Gospel's trumpet-call!

Arise, ye ransomed hosts, in consecration,
And pay the Lord your vows in word and deed!
Harken in awe to Hist'ry's proclamation:
"The blood of martyrs is the Church's seed!"
They did not die in vain by sword and fire,
Who pledged their troth to Jesus unto death,
Who praised His Name upon the fun'ral pyre,
And entered glory, saved by grace, through faith!

No cross, no crown! The trumpet-call has sounded!
O Church of Jesus, keep His doctrine pure!
On Scripture's Rock securely Thou art grounded!
His Holy Word forever shall endure!
What though the battlefields have oft been gory?
The lurid gates of hell shall not prevail!
Lift high the banner of the King of Glory,
And fight the fight of Faith when foes assail!

Arise, ye pilgrims to the realm eternal!
The standard of the Crucified unfurl!
His Word illumes your path with Light supernal!
A crown awaits you at the Gates of Pearl!
Though hot the battle, sore the tribulation,
Heed not a godless, sneering world's complaints!
Led by the Captain of your soul's salvation,
Fight for the Faith delivered to the saints!

Arise, ye children of the Reformation!
Tell all the world "The Just shall live by faith!"
Proclaim the Gospel-truth to ev'ry nation!
Be loyal to your Master unto death!
In love He promised He will leave you never!
His Holy Word shall be your staff and rod!
Ye victors, give Him all the glory ever!
Indeed, A Mighty Fortress is our God![79]

For "memorial services" in connection with a funeral, Anna composed a poem honoring Rev. W.J. Kaiser, voicing the hopes of a pastor for his flock following his departure. *The Lutheran Witness* reprinted it less than two months later.

A Christian's Farewell

This poem was read by Pastor W.C. Meinzen at the request of the Lutheran poetess Miss Anna Hoppe in the Pastor W.J. Kaiser memorial services in Emmaus Lutheran Church, Indianapolis, Ind., on February 7, 1935.

Weep not, belov'd, when I am gone,
But let me sleep.
My journey was a weary one,
Hills were so steep.
The valleys dark and filled with thorns the road,
At last I reached the city of my God.
Why do ye weep?

Oft have I longed for peace and rest;
Now rest is mine,
And on my loving Savior's breast
I now recline.
The stream of life in crystal beauty flows;
How sweet my slumber, perfect my repose!
Why do ye pine?

My God prepared this home for me
In realms on high,
And all is blest tranquility
Beyond the sky.

No pain I know, no sorrow, no alarms;
I rest serenely in my Shepherd's arms.
Why do ye sigh?

Washed in my Savior's precious blood,
Saved by His grace,
His Father's house is my abode,
I see His face.
Faith changed to sight! On this immortal shore
The precious loved ones who have gone before
I can embrace.

Weep not, belov'd, soon shall we meet
On Salem's shore,
And oh! reunion will be sweet;
All sorrow o'er.
The gates of pearl, the streets of purest gold,
With raptured joy your eyes will then behold.
Oh, weep no more!

Weep not, although 'tis hard to bear
The parting pain.
Though death so ruthlessly did tear
Love's bond in twain.
My God will lead you by His loving hand
And comfort you, until in Gloryland
We meet again.

ANNA HOPPE.[80]
Milwaukee, Wis.

Upon the golden anniversary of Rev. Oscar Kaiser—likely a relative to Rev. W.J. Kaiser—at nearby Bethlehem Lutheran Church (LCMS), a special celebratory service was held. For the amusement of the company honoring the former *Lutheran Witness* secretary and hymn translator, an evening program was held in the school hall. It is noted that "Miss Anna Hoppe, Milwaukee hymnist, read a humorous poem she had written for the occasion."[81] It is not outside Christian vocation to provide delight and edification through humor—merely another facet of the same gift.

This poem, from Anna's personal collection at the Milwaukee Historical Society, is dedicated to a dear friend for an unknown occasion—quite possibly a birthday.

To my dear Friend,
Mrs. Alvina Benzenberg

All the way thy gracious Lord will guide thee,
Lead thee gently by His tender Hand,
Valiantly defend when ills betide thee,
In your sojourn in this pilgrim-land.
No matter what thy daily need may be,
An all-sufficient Christ sustaineth thee!

Be not dismayed; let earthborn fears not grieve thee,
Earth's friends may fail, He still abides the same.
Ne'er for a moment will His watch-care leave thee;
Zealous is He Who calls His sheep by name!
Eternal life is thine, His Blood has bought thee;
Now power can take thee from Immanuel's land!
Blessings abound with Him Whose love has sought thee;
No power can take thee from Thy Shepherd's hand.
Rejoice, dear heart! Till thou His Face wilt see,
Goodness and mercy still will follow thee! (Psalm 23.)

Anna Hoppe, Milwaukee, Wis.

(The beginning letters of each line spell ALVINA BENZENBERG)[82]

Anna seems to have drafted her literary pieces in by hand, then transferred them to the typed page through her work typewriter. Another undated, handwritten poem, located in her personal collection at the Milwaukee Historical Society, exhibits her style in an unrefined form:

The trembling sinners feareth
That God can ne'er forget
But one full payment cleareth
His memory of debt.

When naught beside could still us
Or set our souls at large
O hear us, Lord Jesus,
Thy Blood our sins discharge

If the Law my discharge procured
And grief in my place endured
The whole of wrath divine
Payment God could but twice demand...[83]

An undated tract for Jews by the Gospel Missionary Union, Kansas City, Missouri shares an evangelical poem by Anna, brimming with Scriptural references to fulfilled Messianic prophecies. She very well may have noted them herself. Her proficiency in Old Testament history, both from church and devotional study, certainly equipped her. The meter might be unpolished and the language technical, but this concept of an evangelical tool in verse is remarkable.

"Our Blest Messiah"
Anna Hoppe.

Dear Jewish Friends:
Just before our blest Messiah returned to Heaven above,
From whence He came to save us in His everlasting love,
He entreated His disciples at Jerusalem to start,
And then to every nation His glorious Truth impart.
The Gospel of salvation, God's wonderful Good News,
Was first to be delivered to His beloved Jews,
And e'er since then, His people, who bear His Holy Name,
Have had the sacred duty His message to proclaim,
The precious Gospel story, so old, yet ever new,
Forgiveness, life, salvation, for Gentile, and for Jew.
Obedient to our Master, we tell, by word and pen,
To all the world the tidings of "peace, good-will to men,"
Not only to the Gentile, but also to the Jew,
Whose ancient writings tell us the glorious News is true!

God promised a Deliv'rer to Eve in times of old,
 (Genesis 3:15)
And through the holy prophets His coming was foretold.
Each lamb brought to the altar in sacrifice for guilt
Foreshadowed Christ, the Savior, whose Blood
 for us was spilt.
The prophet Micah tells us that Bethlehem would be
 (Micah 5:2; Luke 2:4-7)
The birth-place of Messiah, who'd set His people free.
Hosea in the spirit heard God, the Holy One (Hosea 11:1)
Call out of distant Egypt His Own begotten Son.
 (Matthew 2:20-21)

Isaiah tells us clearly, in words by God inspired,
  (Isaiah 7:14)
That He'd be of a virgin born, the Savior long-desired.
  (Luke 1:30-35)

That He would heal the lame, the deaf, give sight
  unto the blind, (Isaiah 35:5)
Console the broken-hearted ones, the captive's cords
  unbind. (Isaiah 61:1)
Again, the godly seer beheld the Christ divine,
  (Isaiah 9:1-2)
And saw His light celestial o'er earthly darkness shine.
  (Matthew 4:16)
He saw the promised Shiloh, the Lamb of Calvary,
  (Isaiah 53:3)
Despised by men, rejected, and suffering guiltlessly,
  (Luke 22:6)
For we, like sheep, had wandered, and He, our Shepherd
  true, (Isaiah 53:6)
Died to redeem the lost ones, the Gentile and the Jew!
The prophets saw Him buried with the rich men in His
  death (Isaiah 53:9)
And, lo, in Joseph's garden slept Christ of Nazareth!
  (Matthew 27:57-66)
The seer Zechariah, in ages past foretold
  (Zechariah 11:12-13)
For thirty silver pieces Messiah would be sold!
  (Matthew 26:15)
That He, the King of Glory, upon a colt would ride,
  (Zechariah 9:9)
And with the meek and humble in lowliness abide.
  (Matthew 21:5)
The Psalmist saw the nail-prints in Shiloh's hands and feet,
  (Psalm 22:18-20; Mark 15:25)
And tells us He'd be given the bitter gall for meat.
  (Psalm 69:21; Matthew 27:34)
"He will not see corruption," thus David testifies,
  (Psalm 16:10; Matthew 28:3-6)

And He will rise to Heaven, beyond the starry skies.
(Psalm 68:18)
He is our blest Melchizedek, the King of Righteousness,
(Psalm 110:4)
Our Advocate, who clothes us with His Own spotless
dress. (Isaiah 61:10)
Thus, from His lowly manger to sheltered garden-grave,
And thence to highest Heaven, the Christ who came to
save
Was seen by holy prophets, whose Spirit-guided pen,
(2 Peter 1:21)
Portrayed in perfect records the Savior of all men.
Ah, "kiss the Son," says David, for blest indeed are they
(Psalm 2:12)
Who, trusting in Messiah, rejoice in Him each day.

All through the Holy Scriptures, we read the sweet refrain:
"He'll come. He came. He's coming." Blest truth, He'll
come again!
Once David beheld Him in clouds of Heav'n descend,
(Daniel 7:13)
The Son of God, CHRIST JESUS, our Savior and our friend,
And Zechariah tells us, His holy Feet shall stand
(Zechariah 14:4)
Upon the Mount of Olives, in yonder Holy Land.
He'll show His waiting people His nail-scarred Hands
again, (Zechariah 13:6)
Hands that will hold the scepter when as a King He'll reign.
His chosen Bride is longing to meet Him in the air,
(1 Thessalonians 4:17)
With Him His kingdom-splendors and glorious throne
to share.
Just as His Zion waited for Him in times of old,
His people now are waiting His glory to behold.
The signs are multiplying, declaring He is near,
And soon in yonder Heavens Messiah shall appear.
The King we are awaiting is your Messiah too,
The Lord of Lords, CHRIST JESUS, *and He is still a Jew!*

Once in prophetic vision, beloved Daniel (Daniel 2:44)
Saw the eternal Kingdom of our Immanuel.
Mountains shall burst asunder, the trembling earth shall
   quake,
When as a potter's vessel earth's kingdoms He shall
   break. (Psalm 2:9)
HIS is the Throne of David; to HIM all knees shall bow.
   (Philippians 2:10)
O why delay? Adore Him! Hail Him your Savior now!
The Lily of the Valley, the Morning Star is He,
The Chief among Ten Thousand, and His redeemed are we.
O just to know the Savior, all earthly wealth transcends,
And since He loves you dearly, we love you, Jewish
   Friends!

"Come, even so, come quickly," implores beloved John.
Thus ends the Holy Bible we build our hopes upon.
"Yea, surely I come quickly!" Come Jesus, quickly come,
Come in the clouds of Heaven and take Thy people Home!
O will you not accept Him, and join us in this prayer,
And with your blest Messiah His Throne and Kingdom
   share?

We will not cease to love you, we will not cease to pray
For the peace of His Jerusalem, till we behold His day!
   (Psalm 122:6; Isaiah 61:7)
Oh, how it would delight us, if in His mansion fair
We would behold you, Jewish friends, the answer to our
   prayer!

You will learn more about this wonderful Savior, our
Messiah and yours, by calling at, or writing to the address
below.[84]

One is resigned to wonder how many more of these literary re-
freshments existed, and how many still remain today. These morsels
illustrate the range of ways Anna's vocation as a Christian writer
manifested itself, but the fact that this small sample presents such
diversity hints at its proliferation during her lifetime.

Songs of the Church Year (1928)

Composition of the *Songs of the Church Year* hymns began as early as 1919, beginning with the Gospel texts of every other Sunday through 1920. Anna's 1921 poems are primarily occasional, and 1922 sees a concentration on uncited German translations. But nearing the end of the year, Epistle hymns make an appearance, steadily increasing over the next three years. *The Northwestern Lutheran* featured twenty-three original hymns and translations by Anna in 1925, preceding twenty-five more in 1926. Almost every issue held a new hymn. Once each Sunday in the church year was provided for in translation or Anna's verse, her name drifted from the front page for a time.

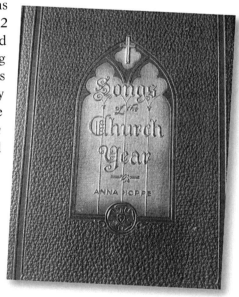

What were Anna's hymn-writing experiences like?

Experiences! O, there have been songs of joy bubbling forth when the sun smiled upon my path, there have been "songs in the day of the East Wind," and when the Lord desired "spices from His garden" as portrayed in the Songs of Solomon, He sent the North and South winds too! Some of the hymns were penned on the way to and from work, and to and from Church, some of the words came "out of the somewhere into the here" so rapidly that I had to abbreviate them lest the dictator get ahead of me. Others required a more patient courting of the Muse. Especially is this true in some of the translations, when I found it as difficult for these old German bards to "speak English" as Luther found it when he wanted the ancient Hebrew writers to speak German! But there are happy exceptions. At times some of the tenderness and warmth and "Innigkeit" [poignant intimacy/Ed.]is lost in the translation of Scandinavian and German hymns into English, but the faith of the fathers is there, in the language of the children![85]

Anna explains further how her life experiences under the Christian cross drew out her lyrical, hymnic voice. Composing—and singing—verses that foretold of eternal hope cheered her wearisome travel.

The burden of a touching song in an old hymn-book is to "give the world the smile and tell Jesus the rest." But nevertheless it is true that "our saddest songs are they that tell of saddest thoughts." It is only crushed flower petals that distill perfume, only pressed grapes that yield wine. There are personal experiences in the lives of all believers too sacred to disclose, which never flow forth from the pen, but I am sure that Luther and Gerhard and Wallin and Wesley and Watts and the other larks and nightingales of hymnody gave us a priceless heritage in what they chose to reveal. How the old melodies and the words wedded to them grip the heart! When the days are dark I need but turn to the keyboard of the old Hamilton Melodeon. Like Dr. Hult's piano, that organ has an understanding heart![86]

On July 5, 1928, Augustana Book Concern released *Songs of the Church Year*, one of only fourteen books printed for that calendar year.[87] Recipients of the July 7 issue of *The Lutheran Companion* were greeted with Anna's portrait and the opening verses of the first hymn on the cover, with a short description on the inleaf.

A Spiritual Singer of Note

The readers of THE LUTHERAN COMPANION are already familiar with the name of Anna Hoppe, partly because of the number of hymns that she has contributed to our new Hymnal and partly for her songs that have appeared from time to time in these columns. But few have had the opportunity to meet her face to face and in that way learn to know her personality. In this issue of the COMPANION we have the privilege of presenting to you the picture of Miss Hoppe, thus giving you an opportunity to recognize, though you may never meet her personally, a woman that you have already learned to know and to admire and love through her songs. It is needless for us to begin to describe this sweet singer of the Lutheran Church and to endeavor to evaluate her lyric productions. Her verse must be read or rather sung in order to be rightly appreciated. Miss Hoppe sings as an avocation. She earns her support by her hands and strews her songs about her without any thought of remuneration. She sings, in the first place, because she loves to sing and, in the second place, because she feels that in doing so she can serve the Lord and the Church which she dearly loves.

During the past year many, if not all, of her hymns, for her songs are hymns in the best sense, have appeared in The Northwest [sic] Lutheran and in THE LUTHERAN COMPANION. These hymns have now been gathered into a neat and attractive volume that has just left the presses of the Augustana Book Concern. The title of this book is "Songs of the Church Year. Hymns on the Gospel and Epistle Texts and Other Songs." The hymns naturally are divided according to the divisions of the Church Year. There are nineteen hymns for the Advent, Christmas, and New Year season, twenty for the Epiphany season, thirty-seven for the Passion, Eastertide, Ascension, and Pentecost season, fifty-eight for the Trinity season, and thirty-four hymns on the Sacraments, the Creed, etc. In addition, the volume contains eighteen Morning and Evening and Miscellaneous songs, nine songs on Death and the Future Life and four occasional songs.[88]

The dedication by the authoress gives us a peep into her heart and describes briefly the purpose of her singing. We quote it in full: "To my spiritual Mother, The Evangelical Lutheran Church, who has nurtured me the Faith once delivered to the saints, leading me to Jesus, the Author and Finisher of that faith, this volume is lovingly dedicated."

May God richly bless this volume in its mission to praise and glorify Him and to magnify the name of our Saviour and Lord Jesus Christ.[89]

During the remainder of the year, the magazine reprinted an attractive advertisement for the book, as they normally did for other authors at their publishing house.

This publication by a local woman was also not overlooked by the *Milwaukee Sentinel*. On July 20, 1928, a brief article announced, "Girl Here Writes Religious Poetry."

A volume of poems by Miss Anna Hoppe, 2003 Galena street, has just been published. Entitled "Songs of the Church Year," the collection of verse is of a religious character. Miss Hoppe, who is well known to members of the Lutheran faith for her writings in periodicals in Great Britain as well as this country, began writing twelve years ago. The foreword to her first published volume is by Adolf Hult, D.D., of Augustana Theological seminary.

Miss Hoppe is employed by the Mueller Furnace company.[90]

Graebner's review in *The Lutheran Witness* was highly complimentary. For $1.60, one could order a copy through Concordia Publishing House.

The expected has happened. A lover of good religious poetry—it happens to be Prof. Adolf Hult of the Augustana Synod—has encouraged Miss Anna Hoppe

{Wisconsin Synod) to publish her religious songs in book form. For a number of years they have been appearing in *The Northwestern Lutheran* and have been favorably commented upon and widely reprinted. They are chiefly songs suggested by the Gospel and Epistle lessons of the church year. Many of them are lyrics of more than ordinary merit. True hymns, suitable for congregational worship and characterized by a devout, prayerful spirit. Every hymnological form of meter and rhyme is represented. We believe with Professor Hult that many of these songs will pass into the hymnology of the Lutheran Church and into that of the Church Universal. The book is well printed and is beautifully bound in semiflexible cover. The price is not too high.[91]

The American Lutheran supplied the following concise but glowing advertisement in its August 1928 installment:

By the sheer spiritual beauty and the glowing, joyous faith which shine forth from her poetic writings, Anna Hoppe has for a number of years occupied a warm place in the hearts of American Lutherans. She is a prolific writer, but this has not had any deteriorating effect on the quality of her songs. Many of the poems contained in this volume are real gems and deserve a place in our Lutheran church hymnals. Anna Hoppe sings from a heart that is aglow with love for her Savior and she has been endowed in a most marked degree with the faculty of giving noble expression to her heart's sentiments. The Index gives the first lines of the songs with the tunes to which they may be sung. The physical makeup of the book is most attractive and one is rather surprised that it is offered at so low a price. It is a most appropriate gift book.[92]

The Lutheran Companion shared a hymn from Anna's compendium on August 14, 1928, entitled "Maranatha" (the Epistle hymn for the Twenty-seventh Sunday after Trinity). Hult prefaces the sample with a complimentary promotion:

This is one of many hymns of American Lutheranism's doubtlessly best hymnist, Miss Anna Hoppe of Milwaukee, Wis., who soon has completed a series of hymns on all the Gospels of the Church Year. She belongs to the Wisconsin Synod. All the phases treated with Christian doctrine are treated with unerring poetic power. Her "Ascension Hymn" ranks with the most powerful hymning of our Lutheran Church.

ADOLF HULT.

The opening, invocatory hymn in *Songs of the Church Year* discloses much about the purpose of the book, revealing Anna's musical abilities and context, as well as intentions for the poetry to accompany melody. As previously expressed to Ryden, penning a thousand songs epitomized her literary goals. Her motivation to compose hymns issued from the internal work of faith by the Holy Spirit:

Saved, ransomed, pardoned, reconciled,
Thy Spirit bids me bring
A tribute worthy of a child.

To Anna, hymns provide rest, cheer, healing, strength, and comfort, and she expresses a desire to provide this to others.

Grant me a Spirit-guided pen
To write the message down.
That it may comfort others when
I pass from cross to crown.

Inscribing her literary offerings in this volume, Anna writes how she longs to extend these fruits of love beyond her own lifetime. She concludes with an anticipatory note:

More sweet would be my bliss divine
Could I perceive and know
That in these humble words of mine
Saints worship Thee below!

Whether or not the wish has been fulfilled is to be determined by the pastors, service planners, publishing companies, hymnal committees, and laity of the current Lutheran Church.

Characteristics of
Anna's Hymnody

Practical Application

From Anna's earliest literary sketches to her 1928 collection, several distinct attributes show themselves, rendering Anna's style unmistakable to any lover of hymns. First of all, in her poems portraying a narrative— primarily the Gospel lessons—she properly applies the rules for Biblical interpretation. Not resigning the ancient stories to their own times and places, she understands them as being recorded for commands, exhortations, and promises to the modern Christian. "For whatever things were written before were written for our learning, that we through the patience and comfort of the Scriptures might have hope." (Romans 15:4) The pericopes, bejeweled with doctrine and practical application, are here aided memorably with her insight.

In the Epistle hymn for the Eighth Sunday after Trinity, she relates Jesus' warning against "wolves in sheep's clothing" to higher criticism, "False doctrine, in the guise of Science." The Gospel hymn for the following Sunday portrays the New Testament Church as the Old Testament Zion, led by the guides of Word and Sacrament to her blessed Promised Land above. Also, Anna often links the great Physician's healings of physical diseases with the all-permeating depravity of her sinful nature. The second verse of the Gospel hymn for the Twelfth Sunday after Trinity reads:

> By nature deaf to things divine,
> My ears hear not this Word of Thine,
> The gospel of salvation.

By nature dumb to speak Thy praise,
My carnal tongue doth fail to raise
A song of adoration.
Heal Thou me now, blest Physician,
In contrition
I beseech Thee,
Let my prayer and pleading reach Thee.

Comparing "The Storm at Sea" to sin's internal tumult, Anna describes how the Lord directs her course as well.

Savior, when my faith doth tremble
On the rocks of doubt and fear,
When despair's dark clouds assemble,
Let me feel Thy presence near.
When the billows of temptation
O'er life's fragile vessel roll,
O Thou Captain of salvation,
Pilot Thou my helpless soul![93]

Anna likens the great supper in Matthew 22:1-4 to the call to the Lord's Table. In the fourth verse of the Gospel hymn for the Twentieth Sunday after Trinity:

We have heard Thee call, dear Father,
In Thy Word and Sacrament.
Round Thy festal board we'll gather,
Till our life's last day is spent.

The Gospel hymn for the Twenty-third Sunday after Trinity likewise prays for preservation of liberty, good rulers, and grace to fulfill God's commands first as "The Christian Citizen." Examples of this abound.

Anna explains in "We Would See Jesus" how believers in modern times know the Savior: through the means of grace. After sighing, "Could I have seen," "Could I have heard," for verses on end, she replies to her own plaint:

But Thou dost bid me walk, O dearest Jesus,
With Thee in Thy blest Word and Sacrament![94]

Emotional Detail

In addition, her hymns not only teach the clear, objective inter-pretation of the lesson, but also draw out the emotional dimensions the individual does—or ought to—experience. The Christian should feel anticipation at John the Baptizer's news, reverence for the new-born Babe before the manger and altar, and sorrow beneath the cross. Many hymnwriters may overcompensate, concerned about preaching reliance on personal experience, and neglect using any subjectivity. Yet, it is impossible to separate the emotional charac-ter without sacrificing the "for-you" quality of the lessons. Because these stories were recorded not only for history's sake, but also for the Christian's ongoing edification, it is natural and expected that they evoke a response, showing also the reactions of fellow human beings.

In "I Can Trust the Man Who Died for Me," Anna expresses how Jesus even cares for her darkest sadness:

He can turn my every grief to gladness;
He can grant my heart tranquility.
His blest "Peace, be still!" dispels my sadness.
I can trust the Man Who died for me![95]

"Come unto Me" furthermore explores what comfort the believ-er draws from the promises of Scripture, remembering its solace in years of youth.[96] "Lenten Meditations" explores the believer's reali-zation of his or her sin's weight, following the Savior to Jerusalem.[97]

Marriage Theme

The theme of the spiritual marriage of Christ and the Church, or Christ and the believer, is one of Anna's strongest recurrent pic-tures. Per her status as an unmarried, fatherless young woman, its precedence in her mind should be expected. Compared to the brid-al themes of Paul Gerhardt, Anna may well be better equipped to detail the depth of this metaphor. Even if their wedding attendance is infrequent, women know the excitement and sheer contentment that a marriage celebration affords. The bride anticipates preparing herself in a festive garment and meeting her husband, to be received into a committed relationship of trust, companionship, and mutu-al joy. Though men may observe this as recipients, they will never experience such happiness firsthand as a bride. In this way, Anna's perspective is keener. From the records left to us, it is impossible to count how many attractions, friendships, and longings occurred in her life outside of becoming married. Yet, her deep understanding of love is evident from her hymnody.

Additional examples picturing the blessed marriage of Christ and the Church include "Redemption,"[98] "The Redeemer,"[99] "Jesus Only,"[100] the Joyful Exchange in "He Gave Himself for Our Sins,"[101] "The Longing of Zion" as a bride, and "The Bridegroom of My Soul."[102]

She anticipated the day when the Beloved would fulfill her hopes begun in this life, especially evident in this hymn, published during the height of wedding season.

> Some day with nuptial hopes all realized,
> In the eternal June of Gloryland,
> I'll see unveiled all that I here have prized,
> And clasp Thy Hand, my King, and clasp Thy Hand![103]

Pilgrimage Theme

"While here I plod." This comment, redressed in many examples throughout Anna's hymnody, re-anchors her lofty, idealistic language when it nears a triumphal tone. Faith consists of not a still-standing state, but a continual travel, and the journey is neither light nor brisk. In contrast with the glories of the heavenly streets of gold, footsteps on "earthly sod" are heavy and tiresome. "In the Tents of Kedar" illustrates her dissatisfaction:

> I sojourn on, a wand'rer,
> By countless ills oppressed,
> A thousand fears o'erwhelm me,
> And sorrows mar my rest.
> Foes hold me in derision,
> Friends oft misunderstand,
> A pilgrim and a stranger
> I pine in Kedar's land.[104]

In Anna's personal life, to be sure, she sensed the discomforts of a departed father, changing employments, and her own shortcomings as a writer. Her hymnody does not necessarily pray for relief—a shortened and smoothed path—but sustenance and hope for the road.

Other notable poems exemplifying this theme include "Evening Prayer,"[105] "Our Pilgrimage,"[106] and "The Coming Glory."[107] Yet, this element is included in nearly all of her hymns—wandering, plodding, exclaiming "How long?" while yearning for heavenly mansions in the distance.

Anticipation of the Eternal

The more pronounced Anna's longing sighs, the sweeter the end goal of bliss becomes to her. One hallmark of Lutheran hymnody lies in its finish in heavenly triumph rather than earthly perfection. Nearly all of Anna's hymns, if not all, direct the Christian's eyes above rather than below. This reminds him or her of salvation's sure reward, fortifying with strength. To accomplish this, the author sketches a picture of eternal glory based on Scriptural scenes.

Anna looks forward particularly to singing with the angelic choirs, acknowledging that the saints already participate in the heavenly strain that continues in sublime perfection. "Come join in the song of the heavenly throng!"[108] "To the Holy Trinity/ Worship sweet is given,/ When the saints unitedly/ Pray in earth and Heaven."[109] "Thy ransomed host on earth rejoices,/ While angels lift in song their voices:/ 'Ascend, dear Lord!'"[110]

She draws the consummation of this perfection from beholding her Savior face to face—those continually viewing His glory in heaven cannot sin.

> What bliss to see the beauty of Thy face;
> The joys of Salem tongue cannot declare.
> O let me rest in Thy redeeming grace,
> Till, justified by faith, I enter there![111]

Other notable examples of these beatific descriptions fall especially in the End Times hymns: the translation "The Home of the Soul," and "The Homeland in Glory."[112]

Additional Themes

Other specific themes or emphases, based on life experiences, are reprised throughout the span of her hymnody, such as foreign missions (especially to the Jews), Christian youth education, pastors and seminaries, the Church in the sense of both the congregation and the invisible Church, Martin Luther and the Reformation, and American patriotism.

Use of Repetition

Unlike most Lutheran hymnists, Anna relies on patterns of repeated words. These sometimes provide theological emphasis. Elsewhere they show continuity of a theme across stanzas, and in other places add a pleasant rhythmic quality.

Her oft-sung Gospel hymn for the Tenth Sunday after Trinity exemplifies theological repetition at the end of the fourth verse:

Grant me grace to love Thy Word,
Grace to keep the message heard,
Grace to own Thee as my Treasure,
Grace to love Thee without measure.[113]

Showing continuity of theme, her hymn on "The Resurrection" for Easter exclaims, "He is risen! My Jesus is risen" in the first and third line of every verse, introducing a different Messianic title and aspect of His atoning work. This is inclined to happen in the numerous poems for the ES IST GENUG tune, where the meter demands it.

Frequently, the simple purpose of the recurring phrase—typically, a name or title—is for rhythm, enhancing the meter of the whole hymn. Observe the first verse of "The Church Militant":

The great Jehovah is Thy God,
Church of Christ, blest Church of Christ.
His love bestoweth boundless good,
Church of Christ, blest Church of Christ.
He sent His Son to earthly sod;
The Saviour shed His precious blood
That heaven might be Thy abode,
Church of Christ, blest Church of Christ.[114]

The second, fourth, and eighth lines of every verse in this hymn are identical.

Very few well-known Lutheran hymns use repetition to the extent that Anna does. This technique is more akin to American hymnody of other sources. Advised by the context of Gospel music, many bear a defined refrain section for each verse, and make provision of it in their tunes. In order to acquaint herself with this genre, she must have read modern hymnic literature outside of that used at St. John's, keeping up-to-date with her peers in hymnody. Attuning herself to both Germanic and English-American conventions produced a style much like Frances Havergal's, but distinctly her own in content. Blending elements of contemporaneous hymns from her world with the theology of the old world contributes to a "uniquely American-Lutheran" style.

Synonyms of Salvation

As part of the theology and rhythmic nature of her hymns, Anna often features lists of adjectives or qualities of the sinner according to his or her Christian nature. Sometimes these lists are synonyms. Other times they describe the various steps of salvation and sanctification in the correct order. "Saved, pardoned, justified" occurs five times; "saved, ransomed, pardoned, justified" three times; "redeemed, forgiven, justified" four times; and many similar lists appear. Verse three of her creedal hymn "I Believe in God the Holy Spirit" reads:

Saved, ransomed, pardoned, justified,
Sustained in faith, and sanctified,
How blest the saints' communion!

In all her hymns, even those concentrating on works Christians carry out by faith, she accentuates the blessedness in which they live, thus enabling them to serve.

Associated with this, the "blood-bought" state of the saints comes out in nearly every hymn. Anna often writes with Christ's purchase by blood or redemption symbolizing the whole act of justification. This also signifies its relation to the Old Testament sacrifices. Jewish readers would note the strong Paschal themes related to Jesus, while New Testament Christians sense how their Messiah fulfills the Old Testament types.

Emphasis on Jewish Connection

For a layperson of German background, Anna's substantial usage of Hebrew place-names—sometimes seeming like reaches—shows both her Biblical competency and her passion for Jewish missions.

When picturing God present in the Old Testament, Anna often uses "Jehovah." Sometimes this indicates the whole Triune God, as in the Epistle hymn for the First Sunday after Easter:

In the name of Christ we gather
To adore and worship Thee,
Mighty God, Eternal Father,
Great Jehovah, One in Three.

In additional places, it particularly means God the Father, the first Person of the Trinity. "The great Jehovah is Thy God…He sent His Son to earthly sod."[115] In referring to the Second Person of the Trinity, she often chooses to call him Shiloh ("The Peaceful One" or "The One Who Fulfills"). The Augustana Synod frequently replaced this with "Savior" to stay consistent with the New Testament depiction of Jesus in the Gospels. Many Old Testament references are otherwise mixed with them.

Throughout the seasons of the lectionary, Anna uses a biblical place-name as a synecdoche for the event that occurred there. For example, in summarizing redemption or atonement, she favors referring to "Calvary" or "Calvary's cross"—designating redemption, why Calvary holds importance for the Christian. Christ's act of washing from sins is usually connected or included in this scene. Often, the thunders of Sinai or Horeb—the Law—drive the sinner to find solace in its opposite, the hill of the cross—the Gospel.

Shine into hearts beneath sin's burden groaning,
Who fear the thund'rous roar of Sinai,
And sadly grieve, their wretchedness bemoaning,
Bid them on wings of faith to Calv'ry fly.[116]

Anna uses "Salem"—a rhythmical, shortened form of "Jerusalem"— literally in speaking of Gospel narratives. In application, it figuratively denotes either the invisible Church, or the specific place of heaven in eternity. When this occurs, the context clarifies which one it is. "Kidron," the valley between the Mount of Olives and Jerusalem, sometimes describes the physical location. Alternately, she addresses the Church "Zion" or "Daughter of Zion."

Within the Gospel hymn for the Fourth Sunday in Lent, likening the feeding of the five thousand to the provision of manna, Anna writes:

O Israel, it is Messiah,
Who thus hath multiplied your bread,
The God of Moses and Elijah,
He who Sarepta's table spread...

"Sarepta" is a Germanized form of Zarephath, here acting as a synecdoche for the widow of Zarephath who, along with her son, was miraculously fed by the Lord through Elijah. The only instance in Scripture with this word is the German transliteration in Luke 4:26. (Anna may have accumulated variant spellings from her native tongue's Bible.) "Shekinah glory" occurs three times; first, in the Epistle hymn for the second Sunday after Epiphany; secondly, in the evening hymn "Light at Eventide;" and thirdly, in her January 4, 1931 hymn "I Shall Not Want." The term, though never used in Scripture, comes from the Aramaic and conveys the "dwelling" presence of God. Her ease in handling this terminology reveals her biblical studies.

Particularly, she favors comparing the Exodus with the Christian's travel homeward. "Egypt" refers to the temporal desert of sin, and "Canaan" the blessed fatherland.

With Thy blood upon my heart
From sin's Egypt I'll depart!
By the virtue of Thy passion
Cleanse me, Lord, from all transgression.[117]

The remainder of this hymn is rich in related imagery. "Pisgah" refers to the mountain on which Moses surveyed the Promised Land, and "crossing Jordan" typifies physical death and entrance into divine, eternal bliss.

Connected with this, Anna equivocates the Word and Sacrament as "manna" in the earthly wilderness. Dwelling "In the Tents of Kedar," as her February 5, 1922 title reads, is a metaphor for being separated from Israel (here, the Church Triumphant), for Kedar was a land of exile.

Though esoteric, the frequency of these references shows Anna's education in Biblical stories, as well as her personal interest in Israelite history and missions. She voluntarily participated in Jewish mission groups at her church and beyond, and its terminology certainly arose. To her Gentile audience, this language directs them to the continuity of the Church—they, themselves, are included with Old Testament Zion in the Scriptural accounts, and should realize that they are joint heirs with them in salvation.

Evocative Language

Anna's exclamation-point typewriter key must have been worn and maintained well! Diverging from the calm, passive voice of many poets and translators, she shouts as loudly as an ink ribbon and paper can afford her. Often, these exhortations are interspersed with rhetorical questions: "Do this, Christian! Why not?" Spoken aloud, her words may be most appropriate in the pulpit, declared by a pastor. Nevertheless, Anna seems to evade "preaching" as long as it is printed and in rhyme.

In the Epistle hymn for the First Sunday in Advent, particularly the *Northwestern Lutheran* version,[118] this unconstrained tone shows itself:

Wake! Wake! Ye sleeping Christians!
Jesus calls you! Rise! Arise!
Leave sin's dark pit! God's glorious light
Dispels the dismal gloom of night!
Salvation's beams illume the skies!
From sleep of sin to life arise!
Waken! Waken! Waken!

Reviewing the examples with their *Lutheran Companion* and *Songs of the Church Year* alterations, one should notice that the later editions remove the exclamations Anna adds so freely. Compare the following two excerpts, the first from *The Northwestern Lutheran*, and the second from *Songs of the Church Year*:

He is risen! My Jesus is risen!
My precious Redeemer, my Lord!
He is risen! My Jesus is risen!
What joy this blest truth doth afford!

The tidings on angelic pinions
Are wafted o'er earth's vast domain!
All vanquished are Satan's dominions.
The Crucified liveth again!

He is risen! My Jesus is risen,
My precious Redeemer, my Lord!
He is risen; My Jesus is risen,
What joy this blest truth doth afford!
The tidings on angelic pinions
Are wafted o'er earth's wide domain;
All vanished are Satan's dominions.
The Crucified liveth again!

Another factor in this tone is her enthusiasm toward capitalizing nouns—a trait left over from her native German grammar. As some of her cross-linguistic habits come out in her English, this experience coupled with theological understanding surfaces in her translating style.

Translations

Translations of European hymns were all the rage in Anna's day, but often for non-theological reasons. One could say that Catherine Winkworth pioneered this movement, but, being Anglican, this was not to promote their superior theology. Rather, it coincided with the deep literary fascination for all things exotic, archaic, and embellished of the Victorian era. Reading Gerhardt hymns with this mind, for example, would produce translations true to the mystical interpretation of the poem, but not necessarily its Lutheran rhetoric.

One example of this difference between Lutheran and Protestant thought emerges in how they portray the theologies of cross and glory. In the Christmas story, Anglicans, Methodists, and the like draw attention to the glorious songs of the angels, the trumpets, the wealth of the wise men, and the humble contrast of the King in a manger. Lutherans, uncovering the hiddenness of God's glory through Scripture, see this manger as a paradise, around which the plan of salvation revolves. During Easter, Protestants emphasize the pain of the awful crucifixion, the joy in Christ's visible resurrection, and His renewed physical presence with the disciples. Though

Lutheran hymns portray the crucifixion in its graphic reality, they also view it as the most beautiful revelation of His love. Many remember Pentecost for the astounding gift of tongues, rather than the sending of the Word to all Gentiles. Relating to the life and work of Jesus Christ, especially in the Trinity season, the Reformed gravitate toward the amazing quality of His power to heal and supply physical needs, rather than the greater cure for sin within the Gospel. Equipped with a likeminded approach to the German authors, Anna is arguably nearest to the intended meaning.

Overall, *Songs of the Church Year* collects refinements of hymns already published that decade in *The Northwestern Lutheran.* Where some of Anna's tendencies are more pronounced, they are softened for readability and congregational use. Difficult vocabulary is removed. Exclamations occur sparingly, and punctuation is rearranged.

"A Prayer for Christmas 1931" succinctly contains most of the abovementioned traits. Yet more impressive hymns include "O Come, Let Us Sing to the Lord," "His Birthday," "The City Missionary," "On the Death of a Pastor," and "My Bible."

Much more could be said and analyzed concerning Anna's theological content and zealous style, armed with a sensible dash of inconspicuous wit. It is most effective, however, for the reader to admire these treasures for him- or herself. Reading the beginnings of her work from the front pages of *The Northwestern Lutheran* then reading their polished, refined forms in *Songs of the Church Year*, one hears the story of salvation, resounding as clearly as it did a century before. Paging through these offerings of hymnody, one can sense the longings of a solitary life attempting to address the outside world with the best offering she knew to give. It may appear to be two mites in the overall stream of hymnody, but the Lord and Giver of all perfect gifts knows its hidden value.

After *Songs of the Church Year,* 1929-1941

This small collection of poems impacted Lutherans of various synods and Christians of all kinds, though its wave seemed to evade the Wisconsin Synod. Anna revels in joy at the tides of encouragement that returned:

Among my cherished possessions are the letters received when Augustana Book Concern released *Songs of the Church Year*. From all parts of the country they come, from South America, England, Scotland, Palestine, Africa, Finland, Germany, from pastors and missionaries of different denominations, from Lutherans of different synods. Papers in Australia, England, and Scotland have reproduced a number of them. One Christmas song was sung in a Catholic Church, and two, "Ascend, dear Lord" and "O Church of the Word" have been translated into German by a scholarly writer in the East. "Depression" hymns penned early in 1933, "Undertake for me" and "He Can" have been reproduced by papers of other denominations. Two stanzas of "Just a Little While" comprise one of the monthly meditations of a 1934 calendar published in Scotland. If any of these effusions have spread comfort and cheer and encouragement, to God be all the glory. Hymns are sweet cordials of God's Word in verse, and His should be the praise. [119]

During the 1930s, Anna's hymn appearances tapered off altogether from print. If featured, most were quotes from *Songs of the Church Year*. But by this time most musical dialogue in *The Northwestern Lutheran* concerned *The Lutheran Hymnal*. A *Lutheran Witness* review of the *American Lutheran Hymnal*, published in 1930 by the American Lutheran Conference, noted its refreshed inclusions: "There are also entirely new lyrics, by Rev. W. Schuette, Miss Anna Hoppe, and others. This is a somewhat daring departure from established usage, but it is at least somewhat justified by the demand of special songs for particular occasions."[120] Anna contributed eight original hymns and five translations from her previously published corpus of verse.[121]

After these further releases, synods of all backgrounds met and appreciated Anna's unique verse. In *Christmas Chimes 1932*, an anthology of religious poetry by the United Danish Evangelical Lutheran Church (the Pietistic Danes), Anna contributed "His Birthday;" very likely the *Northwestern Lutheran* version of 1930[122], rather than the *Companion*'s later poem of the same name.

Interest in *Songs of the Church Year* seems to dissipate slowly amongst the *Northwestern Lutheran* editors. Occasionally, excerpts from it show themselves further within the issue rather than on the cover, but original poems and translations are fewer, with none at all from 1936. Throughout the worship committee's reports on *The Lutheran Hymnal*'s genesis, no passing comment with Anna's name emerges, even in the case of her numerous translations. On the other hand, *The Lutheran Companion* published several new hymns, as well as feature pieces in the "Consolation Corner" devotional section.

The following may be one of her last new translations for a magazine, published in *The Lutheran Witness* of March 5, 1940.

A Confirmation Prayer
Translated from the German

Our word Thou didst hear as we vowed to be Thine;
Our hearts Thou didst see as we knelt at Thy shrine.
Father, whatever the course we pursue,
Come joy or pain, Lord, we pray keep us true.

The world seeks to tempt us, the Foe lays his snares.
And sin's vile allurements come on unawares.
Help us to fight as the wrong we eschew;
Grant us the vict'ry, dear Lord, keep us true.

And when in contrition, remorse rends the heart,
Thine own healing balm of forgiveness impart.
Save us and grant us Thy favor anew;
Watching and praying, dear Lord, keep us true.

Lead Thou us, dear Father, and guide us aright;
O precious Lord Jesus, remain Thou our Light.
Spirit divine, with Thy strength us endue;
Till we reach heaven, our God, keep us true.

ANNA HOPPE[123]

In *The Christian Hymn: A Glorious Treasure* by L. Blankenbuehler, originally an essay presented to the Iowa District West of the Missouri Synod, August 26-30, 1940, the author looks forward to the publication of this upcoming *Lutheran Hymnal*, reviewing the highlights of its contents.

> *The Lutheran Hymnal* is also typically American. Of hymns written by Americans of various European ancestries and various denominational affiliations there are over forty in the Lutheran Hymnal. If time permitted, some interesting data could be furnished on these [hymns] and hymnists. To mention only a few names...the gifted hymnist of the Wisconsin Synod, Anna Hoppe, of Milwaukee, of whose hymns much could be said...[124]

Along with penciled editorial corrections, cross-references, and identifications of statements by "Dr. F. Pieper" in her personal copy, Anna noted her printed name with a hand-drawn arrow. Perhaps she did not know prior to this book that the *Lutheran Hymnal* committee chose to include her poetry.

Early in 1941, Anna suffered a stroke, which rendered her unable to work for the remainder of the year. No mention of this arises in Lutheran news during that time. She passed away peacefully on August 2, during the time of the Wisconsin Synod annual convention. *The Lutheran Hymnal* was born exactly two months prior.[125] Contending with his brethren about the Missouri Synod's continued unionistic practices, her current pastor John W. O. Brenner was away during the time of her departure.

The Northwestern Lutheran published the following obituary, written by Enno A. Duemling, aforementioned missionary for the Synodical Conference in Milwaukee, Wisconsin, who conducted her funeral service.[126]

> After a prolonged illness the Lord terminated the life of Anna Hoppe, August 2, 1941, and translated her into heaven. Born in Milwaukee May 7, 1889, a daughter of Albert Hoppe and Emilie, nee Sieglaff, who preceded her in death, survived by a sister Helen, she attained the age of fifty-two years. In the days of childhood she attended the Christian day school of St. John's, Milwaukee. Later in life she became a gifted and fluent writer of sacred poetry and song and well known in American Lutheranism

and beyond the church of her affiliation as a hymnist. Some years ago Miss Hoppe submitted to the editors of the *Northwestern Lutheran* original hymns she had written on all the gospel and epistles of the entire church year, a most difficult task. The Augustana Book Concern, Rock Island, Ill., published these hymns in book form: "Songs of the Church Year," which are much read and used by lovers of sacred poetry. The English hymnal of the Augustana Synod has twenty-three of her hymns. The newly published hymnal of the Synodical Conference has one of her original hymns, No. 419, "O'er Jerusalem Thou weepest," and one translation from the German, No. 88, "This night a wondrous revelation." She has written more than 600 religious poems. Some of them appeared in England, Scotland, Africa, and Palestine.

On the wall of the study of the writer hangs an original poem on the various phases of his missionary activities at public institutions, dedicated to him by the now-sainted sister.

Anna Hoppe never asked for compensation or remuneration for her literary products. Her generosity and kindness knew no bounds. Like Tabitha of Holy Writ, our departed sister was "a woman full of good works and alms deeds which she did." (Acts 9, 36).

By arrangement of her surviving relatives, services were held at the parlors of a funeral director. Her own pastor, the Rev. John Brenner, who had ministered faithfully to his departed member until she closed her eyes in death, presided on the day of her burial at Synod's Convention in Michigan. He requested the Rev. Enno Duemling to officiate in his stead. The officiating pastor preached on the beautiful text: 2 Tim. 4, 6-8. Mrs. Wm. Lochner served as soloist, singing Miss Hoppe's rendition of: "Wie wohl ist mir, O Freund der Seelen," "O Friend of Souls, What Holy Gladness is Mine when in Thy Love I Rest," and "Oh, How Blest Are Ye whose Toils are Ended." Interment took place at Union Cemetery.[127]

Anna Hoppe is now asleep in Jesus, awaiting her Savior. The hand, which has written so many scriptural hymns and splendid poems, will never write again, Our sister is now peacefully at rest. May a gracious Lord greet her in heaven! God be with her till we meet again!

E.A. Duemling.[128]

The Lutheran Companion of August 21, 1941 opened with an extensive obituary for Anna, certainly informed by her dear friend Ryden's notes.

Anna Hoppe, perhaps the foremost hymn writer produced by the Lutheran Church in America, is dead. The end came to the distinguished spiritual poet in Milwaukee, Wis., where she had spent all her life, on August 2. She had been incapacitated for several months following a stroke. Funeral services for this noted Lutheran psalmist, for some strange reason, were held in a mortuary instead of a Lutheran sanctuary.[129] Burial took place in Union Cemetery, Milwaukee, on August 5.

Miss Hoppe was a shining example of what the grace of God is able to accomplish in humble, believing souls. Although she never was privileged to attend school beyond the grades, she possessed an understanding of spiritual truth that would have done credit to the most learned theologian. Thoroughly versed in Lutheran theology, she was a devoted member of her Church. However, she maintained a warm and sympathetic attitude to other Christians and was always deeply interested in all missionary movements particularly the evangelization of the Jews.

She began writing verse when only a child. Later, when employed as a stenographer in various business offices, she would spend her spare time in writing hymns and sacred poetry. Many of her compositions where written on streetcars, going to and from work. Usually they were inspired by a sermon she had heard in her own church. In a letter written to the editor about ten years ago, she gave eloquent testimony to the influence exerted upon her spiritual life by her confirmation pastor.

After some of her poems had been published in *The Northwestern Lutheran*, the official organ of the Wisconsin Synod, of which she was a member, her poetic gifts began to attract widespread attention. It was Dr. Adolf Hult, professor in Augustana Theological Seminary, who inspired her to write a series of hymns for the entire church year. These were published by Augustana Book Concern in a volume known as *Songs of the Church Year*.

Although a large number of hymnals, anthologies, and religious organs published verses written by Miss Hoppe, the most outstanding recognition that came to her during her life-time was by the hymnal committee of the Augustana Synod, which included twenty-three of her hymns in the Hymnal of 1925. One of the finest of these is No. 171, the first stanza of which reads:

"O Father mine, whose mercies never cease,
Whose bounties toward Thy children e'er increase,
Create in me a heart whose tender love
Reflects Thine own, Thou gracious God."

Perhaps the most gripping hymn Miss Hoppe ever wrote is one based on the Gospel lesson for the Tenth Sunday after Trinity, Luke's description of Jesus weeping over Jerusalem. The third stanza reads:

"O Thou Lord of my salvation,
Grant my soul Thy blood-bought peace.
By the tears of lamentation
Bid my faith and love increase.
Grant me grace to love Thy Word,
Grace to keep the message heard,
Grace to own Thee as my Treasure,
Grace to love Thee without measure."

Miss Hoppe consistently refused to receive any remuneration for her poetry or hymns. The royalties received from her volume, *Songs of the Church Year*, were turned over, at her direction, to various charitable and missionary endeavors. Throughout her life, she gave liberally of her meager income to the work of the Church, even to the extent of denying herself all manner of luxuries.

For more than fifteen years members of the Augustana Synod have been singing with much edification the hymn, "O Precious Thought, Some Day the Mist Shall Vanish." This is a translation by Miss Hoppe of a hymn by the famous Swedish pietist preacher, Carl O. Rosenius. Although Miss Hoppe had no knowledge of the Swedish language, she made use of a prose translation of the Rosenius hymn, which was given her by Dr. Hult. The result was a beautiful piece of sacred poetry, reflecting something of the soul's yearning for the great day of revelation, when all clouds and mysteries shall disappear and faith shall be exchanged for sight. For this consecrated Lutheran psalmist the long-desired day of eternity has now dawned, giving fulfillment to the words of her translation:

"The saints of the God, all clad in spotless raiment,
Before the Lamb shall wave victorious palms.
For bliss eternal Christ has rendered payment,
Earth's tearful strains give way to joyous psalms.

"I pray Thee, O my precious Saviour, waken
These hallowed thoughts of Paradise in me,
And let them solace me, till I am taken
To dwell in Salem evermore with Thee."[130]

The Lutheran Witness trailed their earlier notice with a cover-page hymn, "My Church," altered slightly from her July 16, 1921 hymn in *The Northwestern Lutheran*. The refrain "My Church, my precious Church!" only appears after the first two and the last verses, and a new third verse is added:

O faithful one, how Antichrist pursued thee
And how his mighty hosts thy death have sought!
Strong were thy foes, but they have not subdued thee;
For He whose spouse thou art thy battles fought![131]

The editors evidently took the time to arrange a fitting tribute, and the next installment held a lengthy obituary and recent photo of Anna on September 30.

Anna Hoppe

Miss Anna Hoppe, characterized by the *Lutheran Companion* as "perhaps the foremost hymn-writer produced by the Lutheran Church in America," fell asleep in Jesus Saturday, Aug. 2, at the age of 52 years. She had spent her entire life in Milwaukee, Wis.

For many years she wrote hymns on the Gospels and Epistles of the church-year, which appeared in the *Northwestern Lutheran*, the English official organ of the Wisconsin Synod. The Rev. Adolf Hult, D.D., of the Swedish Augustana Synod had them published in book form by the Augustana Book Concern of Rock Island, Ill., under the title *Songs of the Church-Year*. In the foreword Dr. Hult says: "Her muse sings for periodicals not only in our country but in the front

Anna Hoppe

Miss Anna Hoppe, characterized by the *Lutheran Companion* as "perhaps the foremost hymn-writer produced by the Lutheran Church in America," fell asleep in Jesus Saturday, Aug. 2, at the age of 52 years. She had spent her entire life in Milwaukee, Wis.

For many years she wrote hymns on the Gospels and Epistles of the church-year, which appeared in the *Northwestern Lutheran*, the English official organ of the Wisconsin Synod. The Rev. Adolf Hult, D. D., of the Swedish Augustana Synod had them published in book form by the Augustana Book Concern of Rock Island, Ill., under the title *Songs of the Church-Year*. In the foreword Dr Hult says for periodicals not only in our country but in Great Britain also. It is not too much to say that she stands in the front rank of Lutheran hymnists in our land. No American Lutheran hymnal will hereafter omit adding some of her Scriptural and experiential hymns." (June, 1928.)

The English hymnal of the Augustana Synod contains 23 of her original hymns and one translation from the Swedish language. Our new English hymn-book, *The Lutheran Hymnal*, contains one of her original hymns, No. 419, "O'er Jerusalem Thou Weepest," and one translation from the German, No. 88, "This Night a Wondrous Revelation."

When our Delegate Synod met in Milwaukee, 1932, she wrote a beautiful poem of welcome to the Synod, printed in the LUTHERAN WITNESS July 19, 1932. Also for other occasions, such as weddings, anniversaries, etc., she wrote many splendid poems and never asked for remuneration. Money that was sent her for her work she gave to charity. She wrote more than 600 religious poems. Some of her poems were printed in England and Scotland.

On Tuesday, Aug. 5, funeral services were held. In the absence of her pastor, the Rev John Brenner, who was attending his synod's convention in Michigan, the Rev Enno Duemling officiated, choosing as his text 2 Tim. 4: 6-8. Mrs. Wm. Lochner sang Miss Hoppe's rendition of *Wie wohl ist mir, o Freund der Seelen*, "O Friend of Souls, What Holy Gladness Is Mine when in Thy Love I Rest," and, "Oh, How Blest Are Ye whose Toils are Ended." Burial services were conducted at Union Cemetery Her soul has now gone to the home of which she sang in her *Songs of the Church-Year*, page 310.

My soul is bound for Glory Land;
  I have a Pilot true;
On His unfailing Word I'll stand
  Till His dear face I view
My hand rests in His loving hand,
  To Him in faith I cling.
My soul is bound for Glory Land,
  O Death, where is thy sting?

OSCAR KAISER

rank of Lutheran hymnists in our land...No American Lutheran hymnal will hereafter omit adding some of her Scriptural and experiential hymns." (June, 1928.)

The English hymnal of the Augustana Synod contains 23 of her original hymns and one translation from the Swedish language. Our new English hymn-book, *The Lutheran Hymnal*, contains one of her original hymns, No. 419, "O'er Jerusalem Thou Weepest," and one translation from the German, No. 88, "This Night A Wondrous Revelation."

When our Delegate Synod met in Milwaukee, 1932, she wrote a beautiful poem of welcome to the Synod, printed in the LUTHERAN WITNESS July 19, 1932. Also for other occasions, such as weddings, anniversaries, etc., she wrote many splendid poems and never asked for remuneration. Money that was sent her for her work she gave to charity. She wrote more than 600 religious poems. Some of her poems were printed in England and Scotland.

On Tuesday, Aug. 5, funeral services were held. In the absence of her pastor, the Rev. John Brenner, who was attending his synod's convention in Michigan, the Rev. Enno Duemling officiated, choosing as his text 2 Tim. 4:6-8. Mrs. Wm. Lochner sang Miss Hoppe's rendition of Wie wohl ist mir, o Freund der Seelen, "O Friend of Souls, What Holy Gladness Is Mine when in Thy Love I Rest," and "Oh, How Blest Are Ye whose Toils are Ended." Burial services were conducted at Union Cemetery. Her soul has now gone to the home of which she sang in her *Songs of the Church-Year*, page 310:

> My soul is bound for Glory Land;
> I have a Pilot true;
> On His unfailing Word I'll stand
> Till His dear face I view.

My hand rests in His loving hand;
To Him in faith I cling.
My soul is bound for Glory Land—
O Death, where is thy sting?

OSCAR KAISER[132]

Though a disheartening period of sickness preceded her departure, Anna did not fear her death, as she wrote in *The Northwestern
Lutheran* a decade earlier:

Death may seem dark to some, my Savior,
But not, O Lord of Life, to me.
I know Thou wilt forsake them never
Whose soul and heart repose in Thee.
Why should they fear the journey's ending,
Who from the dang'rous deeps ascending
Reach hills of blest security?
My Light, from wilds of gloom and sadness
I will depart with joy and gladness,
To share Thy rest eternally.[133]

Anna Hoppe
in the 21st Century

Her Presence in Lutheranism, 2018

Where are Anna's hymns in 2018? Interestingly enough, though the Wisconsin Synod has essentially remained silent about her output, select remnants still survive in current hymnals. *The Lutheran Hymnal* claims one translation, "This Night A Wondrous Revelation,"[134] and one original hymn, "O'er Jerusalem Thou Weepest."[135] *Christian Worship,* the collection of Anna's native synod, retained only one—"Rise, Arise," the Gospel hymn for the first Sunday in Advent. All verses but the last are included, with one alteration in verse five—in place of "Zion, worship at His feet," it is "Worship at His sacred feet," to avoid repetition.[136] *Lutheran Service Book,* the most recent hymnal of the Missouri Synod, possesses "O Son of God, In Galilee."[137] The worship committee of the Evangelical Lutheran Synod may have passed on the opportunity to include Anna's hymns in *Evangelical Lutheran Hymnary* for the same reasons as *The Lutheran Hymnal*—the exhaustive list of hymns representing every cultural influence. Nevertheless, that neither dismisses the texts' value, nor releases them from consideration for the next hymnal.

Because Anna's poetry lies in the public domain, according to her intentions, modern choral composers have drawn new sacred pieces from it. Repristinating *Songs of the Church Year* and her other uncollected pieces would aid those gifted with writing music with clever, descriptive texts.

Reviving Anna's Hymnody

In order to recount the tale of American hymnody comprehensively, Anna's *Songs of the Church Year* ought to be dusted off, included anew in hymnals and church music histories. Yet, why does it require this at all? Attempting to explain this apart from firsthand accounts is only speculative. Furthermore, multiple aspects of the Wisconsin Synod's culture and Anna's alcove within it may be part of it.

One reason may be preparation for *The Lutheran Hymnal* in 1941. Already during the 1930s, Wisconsin Synod editors set forth articles regarding their selections in *The Northwestern Lutheran*, overtaking the regular hymn column. Perhaps a sole female author for a hymnal was controversial for the Wisconsin Synod. Literary contributions from women were not uncommon in the Augustana Synod. The Lutherans of Scandinavian background were more impartial to women's involvement than the Germans. Even if those of synodical superiority enjoyed her contributions at church, also tolerating her incessant hymn submissions for their newsletters, they might have felt that distributing her hymnal from Northwestern Publishing House would convey the wrong message. Since the initial reluctance of the Wisconsin Synod to participate in fellowship with the conservative Synodical Conference, its leaders practiced caution. At this time, when the synod needed to navigate relations with Missouri carefully, it vested most of its hymnological energy into preparing and translating the future *Lutheran Hymnal*.

Though hidden from Wisconsin Synod's history, interpersonal clashes may figure into her limited presence as well. Anna's strong personality and will to publish her doctrinal views in both poetry and prose might have abetted resistance. In official publications, nothing depreciative is actually said of her work. However, where the silence lies concerning the extent of her work is most telling. Scattered throughout the neighboring synods, illustrious Lutheran figures remark in passing about her accomplishments—authoring at least six hundred hymns, engaging in congregational activities, and eagerly encouraging them and other Christians in their vocations. Curiously, those of her own did not mention her talent as much as they might have, though it deserved such. Rather, her gifts were sown and harvested in the hidden garden of St. John's, her friends, local editors, distant correspondents, and her family.

Her style, indeed distinctive, may have been considered too disparate from other hymnists at its most extreme. As Ryden noted, "They are thoroughly Scriptural in language, although they sometimes become too dogmatic in phraseology."[138] As noted above, for uniformity with other common hymn texts, alterations in language to avoid overemphasis or awkward colloquialisms are needed. In the 21st century, her speech, similar to the King James Version of the Bible, would benefit from an update—some of the word-pictures deserve as much clarity as is possible.

A plausible conclusion is that her friends of the Augustana Synod—Adolf Hult, Ernest Edwin Ryden, colleagues at their schools, and the Augustana Book Concern—found and promoted Anna's hymnody first. Hult, after extending the idea of a book to Anna, may have arranged for the details of its publication, and Northwestern Publishing House resigned the matter to another press.

Regardless of the prevalence of Anna's writing in her own synod, her personal memoirs and items are select and at a premium. Here the long-term effects of vocation face reality. Bundles of saved letters may be tossed; pivotal notes may be discarded from the writer's desk. Church bulletins, newsletters, tickets, and programs—evidence of Anna's involvement—may be considered outdated material. To local acquaintances and those reviewing her estate, her work did not have seemed valuable at the national level, as later hymnologists aver. All in all, no one can fully discover how ubiquitous her hymnody became in its own time from what remains over seventy years later. As witnessed above, in the beautiful style and generous serving of theology her poetry provides, the Church would indeed be benefited by a renaissance of *Songs of the Church Year*, as well as her other uncollected and unpublished hymns.

Anna's Vocation as a Hymnwriter

Vocation may be misunderstood as referring to one specific position of employment into which the Christian is placed. For example, according to the conventional definition, one might say he has a Christian vocation as a teacher, but the roles of father, son, caretaker, student, American citizen, pastor, and so on are secondary, not recognized apart from the individual's career. However, in the Lutheran understanding, vocation constitutes the complete set of activities the Christian performs out of love for God on this earth. As Gene Edward Veith describes, a person's calling might be in a professional setting, as a teacher, yet also outside of the workplace, as a father. Different vocations may present themselves within those callings. Someone who is a teacher may also be a pastor and teacher of religion, writer, editor, synodical leader, and more.[139] Life under the theology of the cross additionally recognizes that God's operations are hidden, undiscerned apart from faith. Mundane tasks, even those too "normal" to record, are often the very core of vocational work. Through them, the most deep-rooted dwelling of sanctification's work is apparent. Martin Luther's "busy, active faith" that does not stop in its good works.

In his sermon on "The Estate of Marriage," Luther furthermore praises even humble activities of vocation: "What then does Christian faith say to this? It opens its eyes, looks upon all these insignificant, distasteful, and despised duties in the Spirit, and is aware that they are all adorned with divine approval as with the costliest gold and jewels. "[140]

The theology of glory might prescribe that, in order to properly enact a life of devotion to the Lord, Anna should have stepped outside her original station to an obvious temporal position, possibly compiling more hymnals, reaping monetary wealth, and receiving due recognition from prominent individuals of her day. Additionally, it might have pressured her to believe that the greatest realization or proper use for her gifts stood in the offices of wife or mother, or something more "churchly" than an office career. Yet, that would have rendered her calling no less important or suitable in God's eyes. He bestowed upon her the gift of literary talent, education to hone it, and wisdom to discern the opportunities showered upon her path. Drawing upon the schooling allotted to her, she opined boldly in defense of God's pure Word, cheered others with her enterprising and zealous spirit, and heartened those beset by trials with an empathetic voice.

Her placement in Milwaukee during the early 20th century, stationed in secretarial work, and endowed with an articulate pen, was not coincidental. Inspiring Lutherans to sing through the diverse personality of Anna Hoppe sounds contrary, but is precisely the manner in which God deems to work. Anna herself speaks of this vocation:

> Let all my toil be blessed by Thee,
> And through Thy blessing may I be
> A blessing to my neighbor.
> Without Thee all my work is vain,
> Through Thee alone I can obtain
> Strength to pursue my labor.
> Let all my toil, O gracious Lord,
> Be done according to Thy Word.
> With grateful heart let me defend
> Thy Gospel truth unto the end.
> Grant Thou me grace, whate'er betide,
> To own Thy Holy Word my guide.[141]

Enriching the modern investigation of this doctrine, studying the contributions of women hymnwriters such as Anna holds value for the confessional Lutheran Church. First of all, women are not under an obligation or necessity of office to supply hymns. Pastors and other male spiritual leaders may be called upon for original or translated texts as a component of their ministry, teaching the congregation. However, females in vocation at home or secular work compose out of a sheer will to do so. Anna furnished poetry as a result of her own desire, not because it was assigned to her.

Proceeding from this, female hymnody demonstrates how historical Christian men and women dwelt in doctrinal agreement. While pastors and confessors announced their beliefs through the Confessions and dogmatic writing, one has to assume that their wives, daughters, and female friends shared them. Studying the theology revealed in their writing marks the inherence of catechesis in the heart.

Lastly, allowing women to speak from the hymnal rather than the pulpit does not undermine the ministerial office. On the contrary, it credits their pastors for fine congregational instruction. Like Hannah's song of thanks and Mary's "Magnificat," rich, didactic poetry by a woman draws on her spiritual formation through the Church. Though Anna and many of her kind could not claim a college education, reading Scripture, attending worship, and participation in the parish educated them well. Without John Bading, John W.O. Brenner, pastoral influences in the Synodical Conference, and yet others in the Augustana Synod, Anna's hymnody might have strayed the way of her Reformed contemporaries, grown weak, or failed to exist. In her life's narrative, the men who fulfilled their God-given calling are most highly complimented.

As a result of her true and faithful performance of her vocation, others in her church, community, and the extended Synodical Conference respected her work. William Dallmann, former president (1899-1901) and vice-president (1901-32) of the Missouri Synod as well as editor of *The Lutheran Witness* (1891-95), praised her in his memoirs.

> Speaking of hymns reminds me of my remarkable friend Miss Anna Hoppe. All her schooling was that of a parish school, yet some of her hymns were put into the Swedish Augustana hymnal and into our revised hymnal. Some of her pieces were set to music by my friend Liborius Semmann, President of the Music Teachers' Association of America.[142]

Flavoring her hymnody and outlook on Christian service is a gentle modesty. Anna's writings celebrated the good and noble, defended the truth from error, and promoted the faith she confessed. No undertones of earthly gain pervaded that goal. She made known to publishers that none of her works were to be copyrighted, in order to facilitate their use in the congregation and home without obstacle. Anna told Ryden for *The Story of Our Hymns* that she wished "no hindrance should be put in the way of any one who desires to use them."[143]

As Duemling remarked in her *Northwestern Lutheran* obituary, "Anna Hoppe never asked for compensation or remuneration for her literary products. Her generosity and kindness knew no bounds."[144]

Her hours of stenography might not have paid extensively, but the periods spent commuting to the office and recessing for a midday meal amassed eternal treasure. By surrendering the occasion to earn an advantageous life, she showed an example of trust and contentment, giving thanks with ungrudging gifts to the church.

Conclusion

What, therefore, stands in the way of original American-Lutheran hymns, such as Anna's? Has original hymnody been "stifled" by undue criticism—or, more seriously, lack of awareness?

Nothing hinders American Lutheranism from giving rise to a great hymnist, inasmuch as she remains true to her identity. The Christian poet who understands the simple distinctions of Law and Gospel, repentance and faith, true Man yet true God, sinner yet saint, "body here yet soul above,"[145] glory and cross—realizing his or her responsibility as teacher of the Word—is well accoutered for this role. This constitutes the "Lutheran element" for which Hult longed, which he detected in Anna's colorful writing.

Anna's hymnal, *Songs of the Church Year,* is not the "future Lutheran hymnal" for which Hult, Ryden, and many other worship committees hoped, for she never intended it to be. While integrating all liturgical seasons and occasions, this book represents only one person, time, and location. The ideal collection would reveal also how this heritage represents the Church's song in every place, from naves of early cathedrals to the Marienkirche in Wittenberg, from the Nicolaikirche in Berlin to Trinity Lutheran Church in St. Louis. Anna herself pays honor to Luther and many other hymnists in her writing, praying that her 20th century compositions might only supplement them with "a new song."

The "ultimate" hymnal of which Hult spoke is not *Songs of the Church Year,* nor Augustana's *Hymnal and Order of Service*, nor any of the others from his day. Nor is it the *Lutheran Book of Worship* (1978), for which Ryden's undertaking of the *Service Book and Hymnal* was the penultimate leap. Not even LBW's vision of a single hymnbook for all Lutherans could ultimately be realized. Churches of the former Synodical Conference never accepted it.

In the 21st century, it would not be possible to create a tangible universally-sung hymnal, but, with God's grace, it is possible to create a strong one. Church unity cannot bring about the ideal Lutheran hymnal, but the ideal Lutheran hymnal holds the potential to unify the Church. For example, there is no way that the former Synodical Conference members (the Missouri, Wisconsin, and Evangelical Lutheran Synods) and Evangelical Lutheran Church in America could adhere to their respective doctrinal positions on fellowship while jointly compiling a hymnal. If they conceded their dogmatic identities and did so, compromise would surrender many hymns of value. Those remaining would not present a holistic picture of the true Christian faith.

On the other hand, if an individual or synodical committee were to craft a hymnal of strong Lutheran characteristics, and by it other Lutherans drew nearer to a like understanding of their churches' historical doctrines, this could precipitate a new discussion of fellowship. In place of a practical or self-motivated ambition for ecumenism, it could then be grounded on rediscovery of shared beliefs.

Nearing a century from publication of *Songs of the Church Year*, what should the "ideal" Lutheran hymnal of 2028 look like?

It must contain hymns from the very onset of the New Testament Church, the apostolic age. The ideal Lutheran hymnal first of all embraces its blossoming from the apostolic church of the first century. Shaping a specifically Lutheran hymnal does not necessarily exclude non-Lutheran hymns, or hymns that originated before or outside of the Reformation's 16th-century German scope. Luther himself revered the patristic tradition of chant, providing for its fresh set of clothing in his chorales on the Latin Ordinary, psalm paraphrases, and other Proper settings.

Furthermore, this book should include hymns from when the apostolic Church was restored —the Reformation. The Reformation germinated not in America, not in England, not in Rome and its regions of power, but in Germany. The first sprig of inception— Paul's hermeneutic of sole justification by faith—was not tended by a gathering of political rulers, a majority of women, or the most charismatic speakers. Rather, the attendants called to cultivate this singular shoot were men—learned German men of all personalities and strengths. The singular tool they developed from history and their own culture, the chorale, is unmatched as a conduit of doctrine and art. Eclipsing this flavor of hymns in a Lutheran hymnal, because they are "chorales" contributed by German men, is revisionism and not to be tolerated. God's selection of these means does not designate exclusivity toward a certain culture, gender, or genre. It is simply what he saw fit for the best growth of the Church.

"Multicultural" hymnody may too often describe that which is truly "multiethnic." Worship becomes multicultural when it embraces more than one time, locale, or person—for example, 17th-century Germany and 21st-century America. However, equal representation of every corner in the Church is not necessary—the insistence for multiethnicity should never overshadow the richness of doctrine. Though it is specific in ethnic heritage, wherever the Reformation-era chorale is esteemed today carries a substance that transcends culture.

On top of that, the collection must espouse hymns that are a challenge for people to learn. One characteristic of popular music is that it is readily appreciated and apprehended—instantly gratifying. Yet, as Marva J. Dawn concludes, the opposite of instant gratification is slowness of learning,[146]and thusly it is preferable to use another form when education is intended. Hymnody that demands practice and time to learn is not easily lost, and inspires active dialogue with the meaning rather than passive enjoyment. This does not imply that the process of learning cannot be captivating.

A well-formed piece of art—such as a hymn—bears a clear message, but also turns the appreciator into a participant. This keeps the dialogue flowing. Well-constructed art is complex enough so that those encountering it need to apply their own skills to the discussion. "Classic" works, encompassing the *Kernlieder* of Lutheran hymnody, equip other artists to take the tradition into their own, reclothing, rearranging, and decorating them to suit the culture and context.

The ideal hymnal must use language that speaks or paraphrases Scripture. The Lutheran church stands firm in that while others may add or detract from Scripture, it lets Scripture speak for itself with its sheer power. Since the hymnal reflects the overall practice of the Church and the Word of God remains its sole source and norm, it must not merely ornament, but cohere and reiterate it. Additionally, this identifies Lutheranism within the preservation of the apostolic church. The church fathers' comprehension of this message receives the same reverence. Lutheran hymnody, as a rule, submits its interpretation to the mysteries of Scripture without attempting to override them— "Holy Scripture plainly saith."[147] With this mind, it does not shy away from presenting the unabridged account of salvation, acting as the Word's companion rather than its rival.

This qualification renders hymnody a type of preaching and teaching, part of the duty of the priesthood of all believers: "Teaching and admonishing one another in psalms and hymns and spiritual songs" (Colossians 3:16). Singing a sermon from the balcony is as efficacious as orating from the pulpit.

Related to this, the hymnal ought to encourage and blend well with the historic liturgy which carries the Church's heritage. To be sure, the Bible does not prescribe a single order for New Testament worship, and each tradition is free to adapt it to the best service of the Gospel message. However, in light of the liturgy expositing the Word correctly, it is helpful and right to use. When the historic texts of the Ordinary are in place around the seasonal lessons, the true balance of Law and Gospel cannot but occur. Additionally, the natural progression of the texts prepares the worshipper to receive the Sacrament. The pastor need not be concerned sacramental unworthiness is his personal responsibility when the liturgy and supporting hymns are in place.

A good collection of hymns points the believer to his or her eternal homeland. Music the believer sings in the Church Militant ought to direct him or her to the Church Triumphant, thusly recognizing that he or she claims heavenly citizenship, though yet unseen. Recurrently, the last thought of the hymn notes this goal, concluding its story with a proclamation of hope. If not—as many other Christian texts—the congregation will acquire an aftertaste of works-righteousness or heavenly joy fulfilled on earth, potentially through millenialism. Eternally-minded language also reminds of the truth that, in worship, the saints on earth accompany "angels and archangels, and all the company of heaven." Christians sing hymns on earth because they believe they will continue to do so in eternity, increasingly joining the "great cloud of witnesses" awaiting them.

Yet, the future Lutheran hymnal must also transliterate this comprehension into the present, ornamenting the masterpieces of distant times and places with art of its own. If it is true that modern American Lutherans still hold hymnody dear, ascertaining its purpose to teach and confess, the natural result lies in crafting more. Those with this sensibility also indirectly preserve the other core repertoire. They consider new hymns not replacements, but responses.

Anna Hoppe's *Songs of the Church Year,* along with her poems of other Christian presses, exemplify the latter. Adding a unique American-Lutheran style such as hers completes the ideal modern hymnal, and as observed, traits of her writing support the other features. Even in the cases of *Kernlieder*, her German translations approve the past tradition amidst a wealth of original poems. These newly-penned hymns in turn shape a picture of the Christian church in 1928, as well as anticipate the future. Her elaborate but winsome style requires attention to memorize and sing but holds words of import. The Word of God as set forth in the historic Gospel and Epistle lessons shines clearly amidst her vivid verse. Reflecting the lectionary, they assist and reinforce the traditional Divine Service outline, even on a miniature scale within the outlines themselves. Lastly, her confident voice consoles and cheers the traveling Christian with heavenly hope.

Through this renewed study of hymnody and Christian vocation, may God send his beloved American Lutheran Church encouragement to serve in her diverse callings and discernment to seize the hidden gifts He sends her way. Above all, may he grant a blessed remembrance of his past mercies to her through individuals such as Anna Bernardine Dorothy Hoppe, and a reinvigorated zeal to continue this conversation with new "Songs of the Church Year," pages from the "universal hymnal" of the communion of saints.

Works Cited

"Albert Hoppe in 1900 United States Federal Census," Ancestry.com. Accessed August 29, 2015. http://search.ancestry.com/cgi-bin/

"Anna Hoppe—1940 Census Record," Ancestry.com, web accessed August 30, 2015, http://search.ancestry.com/cgi-bin/

"Annual 'Missionary Calendar' To Be Distributed in December." *Augustana Observer* XXVI, no. 7 (October 27, 1927). Accessed September 5, 2015. http://www.arcasearch.com/usilaugcd/

Arndt, William Frederick. "Dr. Hult Gone To His Rest." *Concordia Theological Monthly* XIV, no. 5 (May 1943): 363.

"Arthur Hoppe—Indiana Marriage Index, 1800-1941," Ancestry. com. Web accessed August 29, 2015. http://search.ancestry.com/ cgi-bin/

"Augustana Conservatory of Music." *Music News* XXIV, no.2 (August 11, 1922): 53.

Blankenbuehler, L. *The Christian Hymn: A Glorious Treasure.* Ogden, IA: Ogden Reporter Print, 1940.

Braun, Mark E. "I want to be saved in German." *Forward in Christ* LXXXVII, no. 6 (June 2000). Accessed May 18, 2015. http://www. wels.net/news-events/forward-in-christ/june-2000/i-want-be-saved-in-german?page=0,1

Catalog of Augustana College and Theological Seminary, Rock Island, Illinois 1915-16. Rock Island, Ill.: Augustana Book Concern, Printers and Binders, 1916.

The Commission on Worship of the Lutheran Church-Missouri Synod. *Lutheran Service Book.* St. Louis: Concordia Publishing House, 2006.

"Cross Lutheran Congregation: Verses Written to Old Edifice." *The Milwaukee Journal* (June 6, 1931). http://news.google.com/newspapers?

Dallmann, William. *My Life*. St. Louis: Concordia Publishing House, 1945.

Dawn, Marva J. *Reaching Out Without Dumbing Down: A Theology of Worship for This Urgent Time*. Grand Rapids, MI: William B. Eerdmans Publishing Company, 1995.

"Dedicated to the St. Olaf Choir." *The Musical Leader* XLIII, no. 6 (February 9, 1922): 143. Accessed November 12, 2015. https://books.google.com/books

Duemling, E. A. "Obituary for Anna Hoppe." *The Northwestern Lutheran* XXVIII, no. 18 (September 7, 1941): 285.

"Earnest Hoppe—1920 Census Record," Ancestry.com. Web accessed August 29, 2015. http://search.ancestry.com/cgi-bin/

"Ernest E. Ryden, 94, Hymnologist." *New York Times*. January 3, 1981. Obituaries. Accessed March 6, 2016. http://www.nytimes.com/ 1981/01/03/obituaries/ernest-e-ryden-94-hymnologist.html

"Entertainments." *Milwaukee Journal* (December 29, 1914): 4.

Evangelical Lutheran Church in America Library. "Abstract of *The Rev. Ernest E. Ryden Papers*." *ArchiveGrid*. Accessed March 7, 2016. https://beta.worldcat.org/archivegrid/collection/data/309274052

Follstad, Virginia P. *The Augustana Evangelical Lutheran Church in Print: A Selective Union List, ATLA Bibliography Series, No. 53*. Lanham, MD: Scarecrow Press, 2007.

"Girl Here Writes Religious Poetry." *Milwaukee Sentinel* (July 20, 1928). Accessed August 17, 2015. 4. https://news.google.com/

Graebner, Theodore. "Review of *Songs of the Church Year*." *The Lutheran Witness* XLVII, no. 15 (July 24, 1928): 261.

"Helen Hoppe—1940 Census Record," Ancestry.com, web accessed August 29, 2015. http://search.ancestry.com/cgi-bin/

The Holy Bible, New King James Version. Nashville: Thomas Nelson, 1982.

Hoppe, Anna. "A Call to the Children of Luther," January 15, 1921, *The Anna Hoppe Collection.* Milwaukee Historical Society (Milwaukee, Wis.).

_____. "A Christian's Farewell." *The Lutheran Witness* LIV, no. 7 (March 26, 1935): 120.

_____. "Come Unto Me." *The Northwestern Lutheran* III, no. 20 (October 21, 1916): 153.

_____, tr. "A Confirmation Prayer," *The Lutheran Witness* LIX, no. 5 (March 5, 1940): 73.

_____. "Defends Pastor For Not Aiding Food Plan." *Milwaukee Journal* (October 13, 1917).

_____. "A Defense of the Lutheran Parochial School." *The Northwestern Lutheran* V, no. 2 (January 27, 1918): 12-14.

_____. "Dr. Martin Luther's Spiritual Songs." *The American Lutheran* XVI, no. 12 (December 1933): 1989.

_____. "Feed My Lambs." *The Northwestern Lutheran* IV, no. 22 (November 21, 1917): 183-184.

_____. "Go—Tell." *The American Lutheran* IX, no. 6 (June 1926): 18.

_____. "Is the Distribution of Tracts Worthwhile?" *The American Lutheran* II, no. 2 (February 1919): 19-20.

_____. "Is The Gospel of the First Century Too Old-Fashioned for the Twentieth?" *The Northwestern Lutheran* V, no. 8 (April 21, 1918): 59-61.

_____. "October 31." *The Northwestern Lutheran* III, no. 19 (October 7, 1916): 150.

_____. "Our Blest Messiah." Kansas City, Mis.: Gospel Missionary Union, *The Anna Hoppe Collection*, Milwaukee Historical Society (Milwaukee, Wis.).

_____. "A Pastoral Wedding Hymn." *The Lutheran Companion* XXX, no. 31 (July 29,1922): 472.

————. "Praise the Lord." *The American Lutheran* VII, no. 11 (November 1924): 142

————. *Songs of the Church Year*. Rock Island, Ill.: Augustana Book Concern, 1928.

————. "The Trembling Sinner Feareth." *The Anna Hoppe Collection*, Milwaukee Historical Society (Milwaukee, Wis.).

————. "There Remaineth A Rest To The People of God." *The Northwestern Lutheran* XVIII, no. 2 (January 18, 1931).

————. "To Our Guests, The Delegate Synod." *The Lutheran Witness* LI, no. 15 (July 19, 1932): 253.

Hult, Adolf. "The Future American Lutheran Hymnbook." *The Lutheran Companion* XXVII, no. 6 (February 8, 1919): 70.

————. "Maranatha." *Lutheran Companion* XXVIII, no. 33 (August 14, 1920): 522.

————. "Our Primal Hymnal Need." *The Lutheran Companion* XXIX, no. 28 (July 16, 1921): 441-2.

————. "St. Olaf's Lutheran Choir." *The Lutheran Companion* XXVIII, no. 21 (May 15, 1920): 328.

Jensson, Jens Christian. *American Lutheran Biographies, Or Historical Notices of Over Three Hundred and Fifty Leading Men of the American Lutheran Church, From Its Establishment to the Year 1890*, Milwaukee: Press of A. Houtkamp and Son, 1890.

Kaiser, Oscar. "Obituary for Anna Hoppe." *The Lutheran Witness* LX, no. 20 (September 30, 1941): 340.

Kibler Ray F., III. "The Lutheran Bible Institute and the Augustana Synod, 1918-1932." (Ph.D. dissertation, Fuller Theological Seminary, 2008).

Korman, Gerd. *Industrialization, Immigrants, and Americanizers: The View From Milwaukee, 1866-1921*. Madison: The State Historical Society of Wisconsin, 1967.

Library of Congress Copyright Office. *Catalog of Copyright Entries: Musical compositions, Part 3*. Washington: United States Government Office, 1941.

_____. "Hoppe, Anna," *Catalog of Copyright Entries, New Series: 1929, Part 1.* Washington, D.C.: United States Government Printing Office, 1930.

Lueker, Erwin L., ed. *Lutheran Cyclopedia.* St. Louis: Concordia Publishing House, 1975.

Luther, Martin. *Luther's Works.* American Edition. 55 vols. Jaroslav Pelikan and Helmut T. Lehman, ed. Philadelphia: Muehlenberg and Fortress, and St. Louis: Concordia, 1955-86.

"Lutheran Singer is Called Home," *The Lutheran Companion* XLIX no. 34 (August 21, 1941): 963.

Morland, C.O., ed. *Jubilee album for the seventy-fifth anniversary of the First Ev. Lutheran Church, Moline, Illinois.* Rock Island, Ill.: Augustana Book Concern, Printers and Binders, 1925. Web accessed November 19, 2015. Archive.org. https://archive.org/stream/ jubileealbumfors00firs/jubileealbumfors00firs_djvu.txt79.

Mueller, John Theodore. "Book Review of *American Lutheran Hymnal,*" *Concordia Theological Monthly* II, no. 3 (March 1931): 237.

Nothstein, Ira O. *An Illustrated Lutheran Manual, Vol. 8.* Rock Island, Ill. Augustana Book Concern, 1922.

Odell, R.H. ed., *Official Directory of Corporations of Milwaukee, Wisconsin* Milwaukee: Odell and Owen, 1904.

Olson, Ernst W., Anders Schoen, and Martin J. Engberg, *History of the Swedes, Part I.* Chicago: The Engberg- Holmberg Publishing Company, 1908.

"Otto Hoppe—1920 Census Record," MooseRoots.com. Web accessed August 29, 2015. http://us-census.mooseroots.com/l/ 8997423/Otto-Hoppe

"Our Institutions: Minnesota College, Minneapolis, Minnesota." *The Lutheran Companion* XXVII, no. 41 (October 11, 1919): 535.

Polack, William Gustave, ed. *The Lutheran Hymnal.* St. Louis: Concordia Publishing House, 1941.

Ryden, Ernest Edwin. *The Story of Our Hymns*. Rock Island, Ill.: Augustana Book Concern, 1930.

_____. *The Story of Christian Hymnody*. Rock Island, Ill.: Augustana Book Concern, 1959.

Schalk, Carl F. *Source Documents in American Lutheran Hymnody*. St. Louis: Concordia Publishing House, 1996.

Shaw, Joseph M. *The St. Olaf Choir: A Narrative*. Northfield, MN: St. Olaf College, 1997.

Simpson, Eugene H. *A History of St. Olaf Choir*. Minneapolis: Augsburg Publishing House, 1921.

Souvenir of the Ninetieth Anniversary of the Founding of St. John's Evangelical Lutheran Church in Milwaukee, Wisconsin. Milwaukee: Northwestern Publishing House Print, 1938.

"A Spiritual Singer of Note," *The Lutheran Companion* XXXVI, no. 27 (July 7, 1928): 699.

Veith, Gene Edward. *God At Work*. Wheaton, Ill.: Crossway, 2002.

Wisconsin Evangelical Lutheran Synod. *Christian Worship: A Lutheran Hymnal*. Milwaukee: Northwestern Publishing House, 1993.

Worship Committee of the Evangelical Lutheran Synod, *Evangelical Lutheran Hymnary*. St. Louis: MorningStar Music Publishers, 1996.

Acknowledgements

The author would like to thank the following individuals and institutions for their influence and assistance with the research of this project:

Mark Davidson
Arland Hultgren
Gracia Grindal
Dennis Marzolf
David W. Music
Carl Schalk
Marilyn Stulken
Gene Urtel
Jon Vieker
Paul Westermeyer

Folke-Bernadotte Memorial Library,
    Gustavus Adolphus College
Memorial Library, Bethany Lutheran College
Martin Luther College Library
Milwaukee Historical Society
Rincker Memorial Library, Concordia University
    (Mequon, Wisconsin)
Rolvaag Memorial Library, St. Olaf College

Endnotes

1   At the time, the official organ of the Evangelical Lutheran Augustana Synod of North America.

2   Carl F. Schalk, *Source Documents in American Lutheran Hymnody*, (St. Louis: Concordia Publishing House, 1996), 13. This hymnal can be perused online by going to the website of the Center for Church Music, then clicking on "Hymnal Collection Index" and "Pennsylvania Ministerium". [1.32]

3   Anna Hoppe, "Reminiscences of a Hymnwriter," *The Lutheran Companion* XLII, vol. 2 (January 13, 1934): 47.

4   The official monthly magazine of the Wisconsin Evangelical Lutheran Synod (WELS).

5   Frances Ridley Havergal (1836-1879) was an English religious poet and hymn writer. "Take My Life and Let It Be", "O Savior, Precious Savior", "I Am Trusting Thee, Lord Jesus" are some of her best-known hymns.

6   Gerd Korman, *Industrialization, Immigrants, and Americanizers: The View from Milwaukee, 1866-1921* (Madison: The State Historical Society of Wisconsin, 1967), 42.

7   Ibid., 49.

8   Hoppe, "Reminiscences of a Hymnwriter," 46.

9   "Albert Hoppe in 1900 United States Federal Census," Ancestry.com, accessed August 29, 2015, http://search.ancestry.com/cgi-bin/

10 Hoppe, "Reminiscences of a Hymnwriter," 46.

11 Ibid., 46.

12 "Otto Hoppe—1920 Census Record," MooseRoots.com, web accessed August 29, 2015. http://us-census.mooseroots.com/l/8997423/Otto-Hoppe

13 "Earnest Hoppe—1920 Census Record," Ancestry.com, web accessed August 29, 2015, http://search.ancestry.com/cgi-bin/

14 "Arthur Hoppe—Indiana Marriage Index, 1800-1941," Ancestry.com, web accessed August 29, 2015, http://search.ancestry.com/cgi-bin/

15 "Helen Hoppe—1940 Census Record," Ancestry.com, web accessed August 29, 2015, http://search.ancestry.com/cgi-bin/

16 Hoppe, "Reminiscences of a Hymnwriter," 46.

17 "Anna Hoppe—1940 Census Record," Ancestry.com, web accessed August 30, 2015, http://search.ancestry.com/cgi-bin/

18 R.H. Odell, ed., *Official Directory of Corporations of Milwaukee, Wisconsin* (Milwaukee: Odell and Owen, 1904), 355.

19 Ernest Edwin Ryden, *The Story of Our Hymns* (Rock Island, Ill.: Augustana Book Concern, 1930), 458.

20 Jens Christian Jensson, *American Lutheran Biographies, Or Historical Notices of Over Three Hundred and Fifty Leading Men of the American Lutheran Church, From Its Establishment to the Year 1890* (Milwaukee: Press of A. Houtkamp and Son, 1890), 53-54.

21 The more moderate General Synod of the Evangelical Lutheran Church in the United States of America (1820-1916) was organized in Hagerstown, Maryland, by representatives of Synods of Pennsylvania, New York, North Carolina, Maryland, and Virginia. (The New York Synod did not sign the constitution until 1837.) The more conservative Wisconsin Evangelical Lutheran Synod was founded in 1850 in Milwaukee, Wisconsin. In 1872 it joined with the Missouri, Illinois, Ohio, Minnesota, and Norwegian synods in forming the Synodical Conference which produced *The Lutheran Hymnal* in 1941. WELS withdrew from the Synodical Conference in 1963.

22 During most of Anna's career, her synod was officially named the "Evangelical Lutheran Joint Synod of Wisconsin and Other States." Its partner in the Synodical Conference bore the title "Evangelical Lutheran Synod of Missouri, Ohio, and other States." Here they will be referred to as the Wisconsin and Missouri Synods, respectively.

23 *Souvenir of the Ninetieth Anniversary of the Founding of St. John's Evangelical Lutheran Church in Milwaukee, Wisconsin* (Milwaukee: Northwestern Publishing House Print, 1938), 15.

24 Hoppe, "Reminiscences of a Hymnwriter," 46.

25 Dallmann, in addition to being English synod president, synod vice-president, and *Lutheran Witness* editor, also served as a pastor at Mount Olive Lutheran (Missouri Synod) in Milwaukee (1905-1940), not far from St. John's. It is almost definite that they associated in person.

26 "Entertainments," *Milwaukee Journal* (December 29, 1914): 4.

27 Hoppe, "Reminiscences of a Hymnwriter," 46.

28 Anna Hoppe, "In Memoriam," *The Guardian of Liberty* IX, no. 3 (1923): 21-22.

29 Anna Hoppe, "Not Earthly Glory," *Former Catholics For Christ*'s Geocities page, web accessed January 9, 2016, http://www.oocities.org/fcfc.geo/poem4.

30 Hoppe, "Reminiscences of a Hymnwriter," 46-47.

31 Anna Hoppe, "October 31," *The Northwestern Lutheran* III, no. 19 (October 7, 1916): 150.

32 Anna Hoppe, "Defends Pastor for Not Aiding Food Plan." *Milwaukee Journal* (October 13, 1917): 5.

33 Anna Hoppe, "Feed My Lambs," *The Northwestern Lutheran* IV, no. 22 (November 21, 1917): 183-184.

34 Anna Hoppe, "A Defense of The Lutheran Parochial School," *The Northwestern Lutheran* V, no. 2 (January 27, 1918): 12-14.

35 Mark E. Braun, "I want to be saved in German," *Forward in Christ* LXXXVII, no. 6 (June 2000). http://www.wels.net/news-events/forward-in-christ/june-2000/i-want-be-saved-in-german?page=0,1

36 Anna Hoppe, "Is the Gospel of the First Century Too Old-Fashioned for the Twentieth?," *The Northwestern Lutheran* V, no. 8 (April 21, 1918): 59-61.

37 Anna Hoppe, "Is the Distribution of Tracts Worthwhile?" *The American Lutheran* II, no. 2 (February 1919): 19-20.

38 Anna Hoppe, "Thoughts on the Death of Haeckel," *The Northwestern Lutheran* VI, no. 25 (December 14, 1919): 197-198.

39 In 1962, this merged with Augustana Theological Seminary to become the Lutheran School of Theology at Chicago.

40 *Catalog of Augustana College and Theological Seminary, Rock Island, Illinois, 1915-16* (Rock Island, Ill.: Augustana Book Concern, Printers and Binders, 1916), 6.

41 Ernst W. Olson, Anders Schoen, and Martin J. Engberg, *History of the Swedes, Part I* (Chicago: The Engberg- Holmberg Publishing Company, 1908), 751.

42 "Augustana Conservatory of Music." *Music News* XXIV, no.2 (August 11, 1922): 53.

43 C.O. Morland, ed., *Jubilee album for the seventy-fifth anniversary of the First Ev. Lutheran Church, Moline, Illinois* (Rock Island, Ill.: Augustana Book Concern, Printers and Binders, 1925), accessed November 19, 2015, Archive.org. https://archive.org/stream/jubileealbumfors00firs/jubileealbumfors00firs_djvu.txt79.

44 Anna Hoppe, "To the Lutheran Church," *The Lutheran Companion* XXV, no. 39 (September 29, 1917): 481.

45 Ray F. Kibler III, "The Lutheran Bible Institute and the Augustana Synod, 1918-1932" (PhD dissertation, Fuller Theological Seminary, 2008), 1-4.

46 Ibid., 4.

47 Ibid., 5.

48 "Our Institutions: Minnesota College, Minneapolis, Minnesota," *The Lutheran Companion* XXVII, no. 41 (October 11, 1919): 535.

49   This poem can be found on the website for The Center for Church Music. Click on "Research" and "Anna Hoppe—Hymns from *The Northwestern Lutheran* and *The Lutheran Companion* (1914-1941)", pp. 102-104.

50   Augustana Book Concern, "Bible Primer—New Testament," *The Lutheran Companion* XXVIII, no. 51 (December 18, 1922): 819.

51   Adolf Hult, "Our Primal Hymnal Need," *The Lutheran Companion* XXIX, no. 28 (July 16, 1921): 441-2.

52   William Frederick Arndt, "Dr. Hult Gone To His Rest," *Concordia Theological Monthly* XIV, no. 5 (May 1943): 363.

53   Hoppe, "Reminiscences of a Hymnwriter," 47.

54   The Luther League was the youth organization of the Augustana Synod, equivalent to the Missouri Synod's Walther League.

55   Virginia P. Follstad, *The Augustana Evangelical Lutheran Church in Print: A Selective Union List, ATLA Bibliography Series, No. 53* (Lanham, MD: Scarecrow Press, 2007), 122.

56   Evangelical Lutheran Church in America Library, "Abstract of *The Rev. Ernest E. Ryden Papers*," *ArchiveGrid*, accessed March 7, 2016, https://beta.worldcat.org/archivegrid/collection/data/309274052

57   "Ernest E. Ryden, 94, Hymnologist," *New York Times*, January 3, 1981, Obituaries, accessed March 6, 2016, http://www.nytimes.com/1981/01/03/obituaries/ernest-e-ryden-94-hymnologist.html

58   Ernest Edwin Ryden, *The Story of Our Hymns* (Rock Island, Ill.: Augustana Book Concern, 1930), 457-461.

59   This hymn is elsewhere attributed to C.O. Rosenius.

60   Ernest Edwin Ryden, *The Story of Christian Hymnody* (Rock Island, Ill.: Augustana Book Concern, 1959), 624-625.

61   Adolf Hult, "St. Olaf's Lutheran Choir," *The Lutheran Companion* XXVIII, no. 21 (May 15, 1920): 328.

62   Joseph M. Shaw, *The St. Olaf Choir: A Narrative* (Northfield, MN: St. Olaf College, 1997), 136.

63   This piece, attributed to J.S. Bach at the time, was intended to be the first appearance of a Bach piece during the St. Olaf choir tour.

64   Ibid., 646.

65   Eugene H. Simpson, *A History of St. Olaf Choir* (Minneapolis: Augsburg Publishing House, 1921): 11.

66   "Dedicated to the St. Olaf Choir." *The Musical Leader* XLIII, no. 6 (February 9, 1922): 143, accessed November 12, 2015, https://books.google.com/books

67   Adolf T. Hanser letter to Anna Hoppe, November 6, 1920, *The Anna Hoppe Collection*, Milwaukee Historical Society (Milwaukee, Wis.).

68 John Jenny, "Review of *The Selah Song Book,*" *The Northwestern Lutheran* IX, no. 26 (December 10, 1922): 400.

69 Ira Oliver Nothstein, ed., *My Church: An Illustrated Lutheran Manual Pertaining Principally to the History, Work and Spirit of the Augustana Synod,* Vol. VIII (Rock Island, Ill.: Augustana Book Concern, 1922): 23-24.

70 Anna Hoppe, "A Pastoral Wedding Hymn," *The Lutheran Companion* XXX, no. 31 (July 29,1922): 472.

71 "Annual 'Missionary Calendar' To Be Distributed in December," *Augustana Observer* XXVI, no. 7 (October 27, 1927), accessed September 5, 2015, http://www.arcasearch.com/ usilaugcd/

72 "Cross Lutheran Congregation: Verses Written to Old Edifice." *Milwaukee Journal* (June 6, 1931), http://news.google.com/

73 Anna Hoppe, "To Our Guests, The Delegate Synod," *The Lutheran Witness* LI, no. 15 (July 19, 1932): 253.

74 Carl J. Sodergren letter to Anna Hoppe, February 15, 1931, *The Anna Hoppe Collection,* Milwaukee Historical Society (Milwaukee, Wis.).

75 Anna's autographed copy of *Songs of the Church Year* remains in the Carl Doving Hymnology Collection at Luther Seminary, St. Paul, Minnesota.

76 Anna Hoppe, "Dr. Martin Luther's Spiritual Songs," *American Lutheran* XVI, no. 12 (December 1933): 1989.

77 Anna Hoppe, "Praise the Lord," *The American Lutheran* VII, no. 11 (November 1924): 142.

78 Anna Hoppe, "Go—Tell," *The American Lutheran* IX, no. 6 (June 1926): 18.

79 Anna Hoppe, "A Call to the Children of Luther," January 15, 1921, *The Anna Hoppe Collection,* Milwaukee Historical Society (Milwaukee, Wis.).

80 Anna Hoppe, "A Christian's Farewell," *The Lutheran Witness* LIV, no. 7 (March 26, 1935): 120.

81 Ibid., "Rev. Kaiser Observes Golden Jubilee Here," (April 29, 1935), web accessed November 12, 2015, https://news.google.com/newspapers.

82 Anna Hoppe letter to Alvina Benzenberg, *The Anna Hoppe Collection,* Milwaukee Historical Society (Milwaukee, Wis.).

83 Anna Hoppe, "The Trembling Sinner Feareth," *The Anna Hoppe Collection,* Milwaukee Historical Society (Milwaukee, Wis.).

84 Anna Hoppe, "Our Blest Messiah," Kansas City, Mis.: Gospel Missionary Union, *The Anna Hoppe Collection,* Milwaukee Historical Society (Milwaukee, Wis.).

85 Hoppe, "Reminiscences of a Hymnwriter," 47.

86 Ibid., 47.

87 Library of Congress Copyright Office, "Hoppe, Anna," *Catalog of Copyright Entries, New Series: 1929, Part 1* (Washington, D.C.: United States Government Printing Office, 1930), 2078.

88 Counting the dedicatory hymn, the original hymns and translations here amass exactly 200 poems.

89 "A Spiritual Singer of Note," *The Lutheran Companion* XXXVI, no. 27 (July 7, 1928): 699.

90 "Girl Here Writes Religious Poetry," *Milwaukee Sentinel* (July 20, 1928), web accessed August 17, 2015, 4. https://news.google.com/

91 Theodore Graebner, "Review of *Songs of the Church Year*," *The Lutheran Witness* XLVII, no. 15 (July 24, 1928): 261.

92 "Songs of the Church Year," *The American Lutheran* XI, no. 8 (August 1928): 468.

93 "The Storm at Sea," Gospel Lesson Hymn for Fourth Sunday after Epiphany

94 "We Would See Jesus," February 6, 1921

95 March 1, 1931.

96 "Come unto Me," October 21, 1916.

97 February 11, 1923.

98 February 17, 1929.

99 Appendix A, Morning and Evening, Miscellaneous

100 November 29, 1925.

101 April 14, 1929.

102 Gospel Hymn for Twenty-seventh Sunday after Trinity.

103 Anna Hoppe, "If Thou Art Mine," *The Northwestern Lutheran* XIII, no. 12 (June 13, 1926): 177.

104 February 5, 1922

105 February 7, 1926

106 "Our Pilgrimage," Epistle Lesson Hymn for Third Sunday after Easter

107 "The Coming Glory," Epistle Lesson Hymn for Fourth Sunday after Trinity

108 "A Jubilee Song" November 7, 1917

109 "The Efficacy of Prayer," January 22, 1922

110 "Ascend, Dear Lord!" Epistle Lesson Hymn for Ascension Day

111 "Jesus Only"

112 February 1, 1931

113 Gospel Hymn for the Tenth Sunday after Trinity.

114 Epistle Hymn for the Fifteenth Sunday after Trinity.

115 Epistle Hymn for Fifteenth Sunday after Trinity.

116 Epistle Hymn for the Sixth Sunday after Epiphany.

117 Epistle Hymn for Easter Sunday.

118 "Call to Repentance," December 10, 1922.

119 Hoppe, "Reminiscences of a Hymnwriter," 47.

120 John Theodore Mueller, "Book Review of *American Lutheran Hymnal*," *Concordia Theological Monthly* II, no. 3 (March 1931): 237.

121 Lutheran Intersynodical Hymnal Committee. *American Lutheran Hymnal*. Music Edition. Columbus, OH: The Lutheran Book Concern, 1930.

122 "His Birthday," December 21, 1930

123 Anna Hoppe, tr., "A Confirmation Prayer," *The Lutheran Witness* LIX, no. 5 (March 5, 1940): 73.

124 L. Blankenbuehler, *The Christian Hymn: A Glorious Treasure* (Ogden, IA: Ogden Reporter Print, 1940), 56.

125 Library of Congress Copyright Office. *Catalog of Copyright Entries: Musical compositions, Part 3* (Washington: United States Government Office, 1941), 943.

126 Erwin L. Lueker, ed. "Duemling, Enno A.," *Lutheran Cyclopedia* (St. Louis: Concordia Publishing House, 1975), 248.

127 Union Cemetery was a joint site of both St. John's and Grace Church, located northwest of St. John's about three miles.

128 E. A. Duemling, "Obituary for Anna Hoppe," *The Northwestern Lutheran* XXVIII, no. 18 (September 7, 1941): 285.

129 The Augustana Synod may not have been aware that the Wisconsin Synod convention occurred at the time of Anna's death. Those who would have otherwise officiated were in Saginaw, Michigan.

130 "Lutheran Singer is Called Home," *The Lutheran Companion* XLIX no. 34 (August 21, 1941): 963.

131 Anna Hoppe, "The Church," *The Lutheran Witness* LX, no. 19 (September 16, 1941): 313.

132 Oscar Kaiser, "Obituary for Anna Hoppe," *The Lutheran Witness* LX, no. 20 (September 30, 1941): 340.

133 Anna Hoppe, "There Remaineth A Rest To The People of God," *The Northwestern Lutheran* XVIII, no. 2 (January 18, 1931):17.

134 William Gustave Polack, ed., *The Lutheran Hymnal* (St. Louis: Concordia Publishing House, 1941), no. 88.

135 Ibid., 419.

136 Wisconsin Evangelical Lutheran Synod, *Christian Worship: A Lutheran Hymnal* (Milwaukee: Northwestern Publishing House, 1993), no. 30.

137 The Commission on Worship of the Lutheran Church-Missouri Synod, *Lutheran Service Book* (St. Louis: Concordia Publishing House, 2006), no. 841.

138 Ryden, *The Story of Our Hymns*, 458.

139 Gene Edward Veith, *God At Work* (Wheaton, Ill.: Crossway, 2002), 48.

140 Martin Luther, "The Estate of Marriage (1522)," in *LW* 45:39-40.

141 Gospel Hymn for Fifth Sunday after Trinity.

142 William Dallmann, *My Life* (St. Louis: Concordia Publishing House, 1945), 107.

143 Ryden, *The Story of Our Hymns*, 458.

144 Enno A. Duemling, "Obituary for Anna Hoppe," *The Northwestern Lutheran* XXVIII, no. 18 (September 7, 1941): 285.

145 Worship Committee of the Evangelical Lutheran Synod, *Evangelical Lutheran Hymnary* (St. Louis: MorningStar Music Publishers, 1996), no. 236:1.

146 Marva J. Dawn, *Reaching Out Without Dumbing Down: A Theology of Worship for This Urgent Time* (Grand Rapids, MI: William B. Eerdmans Publishing Company, 1995), 111.

147 Worship Committee of the Evangelical Lutheran Synod, *Evangelical Lutheran Hymnary* (St. Louis: MorningStar Music Publishers, 1996), no. 343:4.